Eleanor of Aquitaine

Medieval Queen

Eleanor of Aquitaine

Medieval Queen

Kerrily Sapet

MORGAN
REYNOLDS
PUBLISHING

Greensboro, North Carolina

European Queens

Eleanor of Aquitaine
Elizabeth I
Queen Isabella
Catherine the Great
Marie Antoinette
Queen Victoria
Catherine de' Medici

ELEANOR OF AQUITAINE: MEDIEVAL QUEEN

Library of Congress Cataloging-in-Publication Data

Sapet, Kerrily, 1972-
   Eleanor of Aquitaine : medieval queen / by Kerrily Sapet.— 1st ed.
      p. cm.
   Includes bibliographical references and index.
   ISBN-13: 978-1-931798-90-7 (library binding)
   ISBN-10: 1-931798-90-7 (library binding)
   1. Eleanor, of Aquitaine, Queen, consort of Henry II, King of England,
1122?-1204. 2. Great Britain—History—Henry II, 1154-1189—Biography—
Juvenile literature. 3. France—History—Louis VII, 1137-1180—Biography—
Juvenile literature. 4. Queens—Great Britain—Biography—Juvenile literature. 5.
Queens—France—Biography—Juvenile literature. I. Title.
   DA209.E6S27 2006
   942.03'1'092—dc22

                                                    2006004865

Printed in the United States of America
First Edition

To Jason, who is both
my chivalrous knight and my jester

Contents

Eleanor of Aquitaine. *(Courtesy of the Granger Collection.)*

1

The Other Aenor

As a child, Eleanor of Aquitaine often rode down from her family's hilltop castle to the ancient church in Poitiers. Inside, away from the hot sunshine of southern France, was the dark crypt of Saint Radegonde. A steady stream of visitors placed tiny wax hearts beside Radegonde's tomb, made wishes, and lit candles, sending light flickering across the stone walls. Six centuries earlier, Queen Radegonde had fled the grasp of her brutal husband, Clotaire, after he murdered her brother. Legend has it that as she was hiding in a newly sown cornfield from her violent husband, tall cornstalks miraculously sprang up to hide her. Saved by God's mercy, she became a nun and started her own convent.

The legend of Queen Radegonde was well known throughout the south of France. By giving up her crown,

The much mythologized Queen Radegonde was a source of inspiration for young Eleanor. *(Bibliothèque Nationale, Paris)*

Radegonde had taken charge of her own life. She refused to accept the fate men had handed her. Eleanor would also live her life with the same determined independence and would sometimes pay a high price for doing so.

In the Middle Ages most people were known by their given name and by the area from which they hailed. Eleanor of Aquitaine was born in 1122 in France, either at her family's palace in Poitiers or further south in Bordeaux. The exact date and place of her birth is unknown. Her parents, William and Aenor, named their daughter Aliènore, from the Latin words *alia* and *Aenor,* meaning "the other Aenor." Soon, Eleanor also had a sister named Petronilla and a brother named William.

Eleanor's family controlled Aquitaine, one of the largest, richest domains in medieval Europe. Aquitaine spread across most of southwestern France, one-fourth of the present country. It extended from the mountainous

France in the mid-twelfth century. Eleanor's homeland of Aquitaine is located in the kingdom's southwestern quadrant. *(University of Texas Libraries, Austin)*

county of La Marche in the east, to wooded Poitou in the west and the city of Poitiers, to sandy Gascony in the south with its rich port of Bordeaux. Clustered in the river valleys were walled cities, moat-ringed castles, wealthy monasteries, sleepy villages, and prosperous farms. Yellow and white houses with red-tiled roofs dotted the lands.

Known for its hot summers, the countryside was a tapestry of silver blue waters, emerald pastures, and dense black forests. Fat sheep grazed in the meadows. Dark red cherries, wild strawberries, sweet raspberries, and purple plums abounded. Beyond the hilltop castles stretched acres of olive groves and wheat fields. In autumn, the forests turned russet orange and farmers pressed grapes into ruby red wines. Its harbor towns exported wine and salt, while fishing boats returned from the Atlantic with whale and herring. Historian Heringer of Lobbes described the land as "opulent Aquitaine, sweet as nectar thanks to its vineyards dotted about with forests, overflowing with fruit of every kind, and endowed with a superabundance of pasture land."

In the first century B.C., the Romans had named the area *Aquitainia,* or "land of waters," for its many rivers. After Roman control ended in the fifth century, a dynasty of kings called the Merovingians ruled Aquitaine until Emperor Charlemagne united a great part of Western Europe at the beginning of the ninth century. Upon his death in 814, Charlemagne's vast empire broke into a puzzle of small, weak kingdoms, duchies, and counties.

Chaos, fear, and confusion swept over the lands as waves of Magyars from the east, Muslims from the south, and Viking pirates from the north invaded.

The Vikings, or Northmen, were the most destructive. They looted villages and churches and killed anyone in their path. "From the fury of the Northmen, deliver us, oh Lord," the terrified people would pray. Despite tales that the world would end in the year 1000, Western Europe gradually began to recover from the turmoil. The Northmen settled into Normandy in northern France and the Muslims moved into Spain. The Magyars' raids ended when many of them either converted to Christianity or were defeated on the battlefield. The centuries following the collapse of the Roman Empire, dominated by the struggle for survival and the lack of cultural advances, came to be known as the Dark Ages.

The collapse of the Roman Empire created a power vacuum in Europe. Competing groups struggled to gain ascendancy. The invaders from the north and east had to be fought back. The ensuing chaos resulted in an emphasis on fighting skills and equipment, which was expensive. Eventually an economic system now called feudalism arose, organized around the need to maintain fighting forces.

In the feudal system, a king awarded fiefs, or grants of land, to the most powerful men in the kingdom. In return these nobles agreed to provide the king with soldiers for his army when needed. The higher nobles then divided their fief among lesser nobles. These lesser nobles, called vassals, agreed in turn to provide a certain number of equipped fighters. At the lowest rung of this overlapping system were the peasants, who worked parcels of land for the nobles. They were provided with protection and a subsistence living in return.

In this system, the king was not all-powerful. The idea of an absolute monarch was a later development. The king could be threatened by the most powerful nobles. Maintaining the allegiance of the nobility was the king's primary task.

Life could be brutal and hard during the Middle Ages, particularly for peasants. But if one were fortunate enough to grow up as the princess of one of the wealthiest provinces in Europe, life could be very comfortable. Knights guarded the hilltop castles and participated in jousting tournaments that stretched over several days. Wealthy nobles held ornate banquets where well-dressed guests ate with their hands and danced into the evening as hunting hounds groveled for leftover bones. The relative wealth of the nobility provided more money to pay for churches, convents, and monasteries where monks shuffled quietly into massive stone cathedrals and filled them with their deep chanting songs.

However, the majority of people were peasants who would never taste peppered peacocks and swans. Their wattle and daub houses (wooden homes covered with a mixture of straw, cow hair, and dung) clustered together to form small villages. Families lived in a single room with a dirt floor and an open hearth. The average peasant

Peasants who worked the land of wealthy nobles formed the backbone of Europe's developing agrarian economy in the eleventh and twelfth centuries. *(Musée Conde, Chantilly)*

family owned a few household items, wool blankets, and iron tools. They might have owned some chickens, sheep, or half-wild hogs. Most peasants tended a garden patch and a wheat crop to help pay rent and taxes. Oatmeal and beer were staple foods for everyone. Sugar was rare and expensive.

Death came frequently, unexpectedly, and quickly in

the Middle Ages. What medical knowledge existed did little to stop contagions, such as plague and influenza, from carrying away whole families or even villages in days. Widespread lack of hygiene led to numerous infections and deaths from childbirth and minor injuries. The often dangerous work led to frequent accidental deaths. The average life expectancy was about thirty years.

Life was tied to the land. If bad weather spoiled the crops, there would be famine. It was not uncommon for the poorest to starve to death. The one comfort in such uncertain lives was the belief that good people would be rewarded in Heaven.

Most castles consisted of a wooden tower, or keep, built on a mound of earth. A moat and wooden fence surrounded an area with a stable, workshop, and kitchen where villagers and livestock took refuge during attack. During Eleanor's lifetime, many castles were rebuilt in stone and warmed with fires, but they were still cold and damp.

Politically, there was often chaos as one noble or another tried to improve his standing in the feudal system. Noblemen who were loyal friends one month could be enemies the next. There was always a deep uncertainty; death and destruction could come suddenly from any direction.

At the time of Eleanor's birth, most areas of Europe had weak central governments and little or no national identity. The kingdom of France consisted of Paris and some surrounding areas. The rest of modern-day France comprised independent territories ruled by noblemen. In a time when land equaled power, many nobles controlled more land than the king of France, but they owed allegiance to the king because he was their overlord. They were expected to pay him homage for granting them control of their lands.

The lesser noblemen in Aquitaine were notorious for the chaotic way they controlled their fiefs. Most of them had luxurious standards of living and competed with their neighbors to establish magnificent courts in their castles. They also had a tendency to rebel against the duke of Aquitaine, Eleanor's grandfather.

Although Aquitaine was a shaky house of cards, Eleanor loved growing up in her family's palace in Poitiers. She could spend summer afternoons in the gardens under shady pear, peach, and lemon trees, the hot air heavy with the smells of horehound and coriander. She spent her evenings in the castle's great hall and courtyard, where nobles gathered on warm nights after a day of hunting or jousting. There were usually several different types of entertainment. Acrobats flipped and jugglers tossed balls and knives. Men and women danced to music from the flute and cithara, an early lute, as candles dripped hot wax. Storytellers wove yarns as court ladies mingled through the courtyards and halls, the long sleeves of their brightly colored gowns trailing behind them. Eleanor was a headstrong girl who liked to stay up late dancing, eating, laughing, and soaking in every detail.

A troubadour kneels in reverence to a beautiful woman in this medieval manuscript illustration. *(Heidelberg University Library)*

Eleanor's grandfather, William IX, was one of the first troubadours, singers who celebrated love and beautiful women. For years, people had listened to battle poems celebrating courage. But troubadours, influenced by the growing reverence for the Virgin Mary, worshipped women.

The songs of troubadours flourished in southern France and popularized the idea of courtly love. Under the rules of courtly love, a pining suitor idealized an unattainable highborn lady, who was often married. The man proved his devotion and loyalty over time before the woman acknowledged his love. She controlled the pace of the relationship, and her wishes were absolute. In this aristocratic game, it was understood that eventually the couple would become lovers. Out of this tradition of courtly love was born the concept of the gentleman and his chivalrous code of conduct. The idea that a man could not simply demand a woman's love caused a stir.

William's court became famous for this new trend in song and literature. By the twelfth century, Aquitaine was a center of western European culture, as poets and troubadours flocked to the thriving literary atmosphere in Poitiers. When Eleanor's grandfather died, her father, William, became the new duke of Aquitaine.

Eleanor learned manners and domestic skills from her mother. She was taught how to sew, weave, play the harp, sing, dance, play chess and backgammon, and hunt with trained falcons. Taught to ride horseback young,

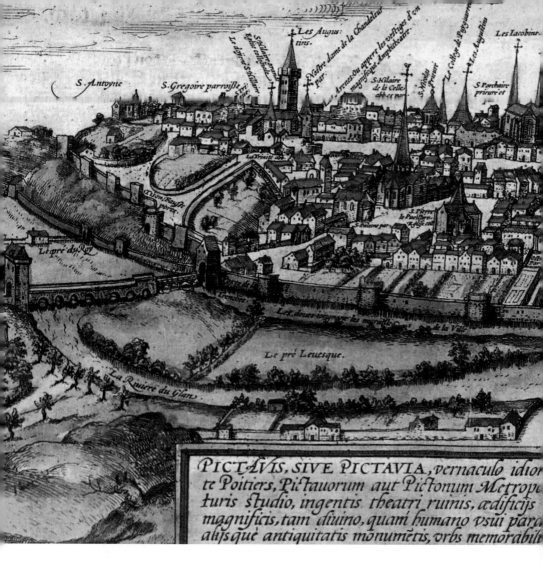

Eleanor's hometown of Poitiers, located in northern Aquitaine, was a cultural hub as well as the site of one of France's earliest universities. *(Braun and Hogenberg, Civitates Orbis Terrarum, 1572)*

she enjoyed hunting and kept special falcons called gyrfalcons. Eleanor preferred riding astride instead of sidesaddle, which was considered to be more ladylike. Most people thought teaching girls to read and write was a waste of time, but Eleanor's family was unusual. Her father saw that she was taught to read and write at an early age. She

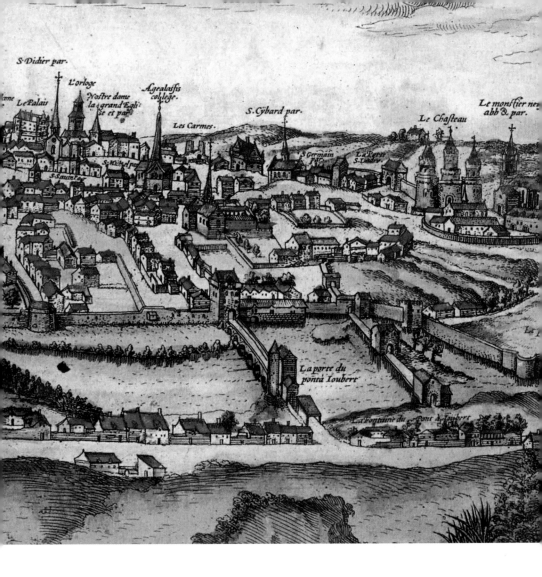

was also given some instruction in Latin, the language in which educated people wrote. Eleanor, like most people in Aquitaine, spoke the dialect langue d'oc, which was derived from a form of Latin spoken by the Romans. In Poitou and northern France, people spoke another dialect, langue d'oil. Eleanor spoke both, but preferred langue d'oc. She was an excellent student who delighted in learning.

When Eleanor was eight years old, her family was hit by tragedy. In March of 1130 her mother and brother suddenly died of an unknown illness. Eleanor was left without her mother's warmth and affection. Aenor had calmed Eleanor, who was boisterous and stubborn at times.

The death of her brother also put new pressure on Eleanor. She was suddenly the heiress to the largest, wealthiest territory in Christendom. She needed more preparation than had originally been planned. Her education was expanded to include the managing of her father's lands. She joined him for extended progresses, or travels, through their territory. The court traveled between castles, hunting lodges, and great abbeys. But her favorite homes were Ombrière Palace in Bordeaux, with its garden courtyards and tiled fountains, and her family's ancestral palace in Poitiers.

During their travels, Eleanor's father would check on his vassals. He collected his rents and his share of the food they produced, and received their renewed oaths of loyalty. Eleanor learned about politics on these trips and at the court in Poitiers and became convinced that governing was not just for men.

Women in Eleanor's era were not only held back by childbearing and household responsibilities; the culture also dictated that their proper role was to be silent and to serve their husbands. The Catholic Church (during the Middle Ages all Christians in Western Europe were Catholics) viewed women as inherently sinful.

Noblewomen were the most sinful of all because their wealth left them more time to indulge in decadent behavior and to turn the heads of virtuous men. "To live with a woman without danger is more difficult than raising the dead to life," wrote Bernard de Clairvaux, a French abbot and future saint whom many considered to be the holiest man in Christendom. Bernard was outspoken in his views about women. He even called his own sister "a clod of dung."

Although Eleanor faced strong societal stereotypes, women in southern France had more freedoms and were often better educated than women elsewhere. Aquitainian women were more likely to have public lives, to mix freely with men, and to inherit property. Women who inherited land were often appointed male guardians, however, and were frequently married off to make alliances with nobles in other territories. Even in Aquitaine a man could legally seize an unmarried woman, force her to marry him, and then enjoy her inheritance.

As Eleanor grew older, she was left to her own devices more frequently. Without a mother, the impetuous, strong-minded girl often did as she pleased, just as her ancestors had done. Eleanor often heard stories of her heroic, bold ancestors. She was descended from Emperor Charlemagne. Her romantic grandfather had carried off Dangereuse, the married woman he loved, from her castle. Clasping her arms around his waist and galloping off, Dangereuse had defied public opinion, the Church, and her spouse to become William's mistress. Eleanor's grandfather's first wife, Philippa, had helped start a monastery run by women, the abbey of Fontevraud in Poitou, which became a popular retirement home for wealthy women and a refuge for battered wives and former prostitutes.

After Eleanor's mother died, Eleanor's father became increasingly argumentative and stubborn. William clashed with the Church over the newly appointed pope and supported an antipope, a man who claimed to be the rightful pope. Antipopes arose throughout history when people opposed the man chosen as pope by the Church's cardinals or when the validity of a papal election was challenged. Because he was a powerful duke, William was able to create a great deal of conflict within the Church and between influential nobles and the leaders of the Church. At one point the pope even excommunicated him. According to the Church doctrine, excommunication condemned one to Hell. Bernard de Clairvaux urged William to abandon the antipope. Outside one of his castles in Poitou, while Bernard said mass, William grew pale and fell to the ground at Bernard's feet, unable to speak. It was said that God had reached down to change William's heart. Thirteen-year-old Eleanor heard the story whispered by servants in the kitchens and stables.

When William recovered, he made peace with the Church. He decided to go on a pilgrimage, or holy journey, to the shrine of Saint James at Santiago de Compostela in the northwestern corner of Spain. Many cathedrals contained the bones of saints, and those who could afford to travel made long journeys to these

The cathedral in Santiago de Compostela continues to be a popular destination for pilgrims to this day. *(AP Photo)*

shrines to pray. Pilgrimages were made for personal, religious, economic, and political reasons. People hoped to cure their illnesses or to have religious experiences by being near the body of a martyr. Some went for the thrill of adventure and sometimes for the opportunity to buy and sell goods. Pilgrimages could be dangerous; travelers faced illness, thieves, and sometimes death.

William knew he might not return from his pilgrimage. He made plans to pass his lands smoothly to Eleanor because he had no male heir. On Eleanor's fourteenth birthday, William's vassals swore allegiance to her. She was now the richest and most desirable heiress in Europe. Before leaving for Santiago de Compostela, William left Eleanor and her sister Petronilla with the archbishop in Bordeaux.

On April 9, 1137, William arrived at Compostela. The day before, he had cooled off in a stream, but the water was contaminated and he became seriously ill. William whispered his will. He gave his lands to Eleanor but worried she would be at the mercy of fortune-hunting nobles. One man had the power to protect her inheritance—Louis VI, the king of France and member of the royal Capet family. William appointed the king as Eleanor's guardian, hoping Louis might marry Eleanor to his son and heir. To avoid the French crown permanently controlling Aquitaine, William stipulated that only Eleanor's heirs could inherit Aquitaine.

The day he made his will, Duke William X died. He was thirty-eight years old. All eyes in Western Europe turned to his tall, slim daughter. Renowned for her beauty, Eleanor was also flirtatious and saucy. But beyond her wit and laughter was a keen intelligence and deep compassion. She would need every bit of her skill as she set out to make a marriage that would alter the division of power in Europe.

2

Queen of France

When William's messengers reached the king of France with news of his final wishes in May of 1137, Louis VI was at his hunting lodge outside of Paris, where he had gone to escape the heat and stench of the city. So overweight he could no longer get out of bed, Louis's eyes were bleary as he sweated in the early summer heat. Although nicknamed Louis the Fat, he had been a hardworking, successful monarch. But now he suffered from dysentery and had mounting concerns about the political situation in France.

Louis had struggled to expand the lands owned by the French crown. He had prevented Normandy and England from uniting and encircling France. William's death was good news that could allow him to realize all his dreams in one swoop. Marrying his son, Louis, to

Eleanor's father-in-law, King Louis VI of France. *(Bibliothèque Nationale, Paris)*

Eleanor would win the French crown control over vast, beautiful Aquitaine. Although his adviser, Abbot Suger, warned him it would be difficult to rule Aquitaine, Louis insisted that the engagement be arranged quickly. There was no time to be wasted. Although Eleanor was heavily guarded, the land was full of nobles who would love to usurp the territory.

The king summoned his son to his couch. The tall, fair, blue-eyed prince was Eleanor's opposite in every way.

Eleanor's first husband, Louis VII of France. (Cassell's History of England, *1902)*

Born around 1120, Louis was the second of six sons. His older brother had been killed in 1131 in a riding accident, leaving Louis as his father's heir. Sixteen-year-old Louis, who until then had intended to become a monk, abandoned his religious life reluctantly. The king often worried about the pious, unworldly prince who dissolved into tears when upset. His mild personality, punctuated by violent outbursts, contrasted sharply with Eleanor's bold, fun-loving disposition.

Louis VI sent a secret ambassador to offer his condolences to Eleanor and to inform her of her upcoming marriage to the prince. As Eleanor's guardian, the king could marry her to whomever he wished. Next, the king ordered five hundred knights to escort his son to marry Eleanor. Chests were loaded with gold to pay for the elaborate wedding trip and to impress his new subjects in Aquitaine. The heavy chests also carried gifts of jewels for Eleanor.

The north and south of France were culturally worlds apart, with different dialects and values. Northerners viewed southerners as lazy and driven by pleasure, while southerners saw northerners as stern and cold. Each area was fiercely independent and resented interference from the other. Aquitaine would regard a northern overlord suspiciously and King Louis hoped to avoid trouble. He warned his son to restrain his temper and not to give the people in the south an excuse to rebel.

On June 18, 1137, young Louis left Paris in the blazing heat, his entourage traveling under fluttering blue and gold banners. He knew little about the high-spirited girl who would become his wife. He was not ready to be dazzled by her elegant clothes and jewelry, the auburn braids that fell to her waist, or her mischievous smile. All he knew was that her lands would more than double the size of the French kingdom.

Louis's entourage slowly journeyed south, seeking shelter from the intense sun during the day and traveling in the cool of night. Even so, their food supplies spoiled in the heat. News of the prince's wedding tour spread rapidly. On the morning of July 11 the travelers arrived at Bordeaux and pitched their colorful tents beside the river outside the city. By noon, when Eleanor first laid eyes on her future husband, the atmosphere was like a carnival.

Most marriages among the nobility in the Middle

The Atlantic port city of Bordeaux, where Louis and Eleanor were married. *(Braun and Hogenberg,* Civitates Orbis Terrarum, *1572)*

Ages were arranged. Kings and noblemen married rich widows and heiresses such as Eleanor for territorial and political gains rather than love. Once married, a woman's property rights were transferred to her husband, to whom she owed complete obedience. Each husband enforced his wife's obedience as he saw fit; wife beating was common. Occasionally, a woman did control lands, farms, and businesses, but rarely. It was even less common for women to exercise political power.

Eleanor and Louis were luckier than many medieval couples who usually met for the first time at the altar. They had two weeks to get acquainted as Eleanor's vassals reluctantly trickled to Bordeaux to attend the wedding and swear allegiance to their new overlord. On the morning of July 25 Eleanor and Louis rode through the city's cobbled streets, past houses draped with banners and garlands, as bells rang and trumpets sounded. They were married in the dim cathedral of St. Andrew, surrounded by lit candles, smoking incense, and singing choirboys. The glittering ceremony and wedding feast that followed was intended to impress Eleanor's subjects by displaying the wealth of the kingdom of France. From morning to afternoon, nearly one thousand wedding guests feasted at a wedding banquet, dining on lobster, oysters, cranes, swans decorated with ribbons and green leaves, venison, vegetable pies, figs, candied fruits, and wines. Everyone ate with their fingers; servants circulated with bowls of water and towels so guests could wash their greasy hands.

Rumors buzzed that some of Eleanor's vassals might stir up trouble. Louis did not want to loiter in Bordeaux any longer than necessary. During the ceremony, his men dismantled their camp and readied to leave. As the hot afternoon wore on and the guests toasted the new husband and wife, Eleanor changed her scarlet gown and headed for Poitiers with Louis and Petronilla at her side. Fearing an ambush, the wedding party cautiously avoided castles known to be openly hostile to the king.

In Poitiers, Eleanor was received by cheering crowds. The next several days were spent celebrating. Eleanor organized hunting and hawking parties by day and feasting and dancing by night. During the evenings, troubadours crooned love songs about noblewomen and the men who worshipped them. In many of the songs the women controlled the relationship. This flew in the face of more traditional medieval notions of courtship and marriage, in which men always held the upper hand. The crude, sexual lyrics of the troubadours' songs shocked Louis and many of his entourage, but made the southerners laugh and clap.

People stared and whispered that Eleanor's new husband looked and acted like a monk. Shy Louis was clearly uncomfortable beside his wife and the other daringly clad women who sang, jested, and drank. Aquitainian women were renowned for their elegance and notorious for their relaxed morals. They painted their cheeks, rimmed their eyes with charcoal, and wore exotic perfumes. Eleanor shocked Louis from the beginning. She was unlike any woman he had ever known, but he adored her. In return for his affection, she showered her new husband with expensive gifts and presented him with a delicate crystal and gold vase decorated with precious jewels. It is the only possession of hers to survive, and can be seen today in the Louvre Museum in Paris.

As Eleanor and Louis celebrated underneath the starry summer sky, messengers arrived from France, bringing the festivities to an end. King Louis VI had died on August 1. The monkish, inexperienced Louis and his new southern bride, whom few had ever seen, were now the king and queen of France.

The couple left immediately for Paris. As they

The center piece in this image is the gilded rock crystal vase that Eleanor gave Louis. The other two vases belonged to Abbot Suger. *(Courtesy of Art Resource.)*

journeyed to their new destiny, Eleanor flirted with her new husband. She exuded confidence and charm as they traveled north with her Poitevin court and her sister. But her confidence would be put to the test in Paris.

After entering the gates of the city, Eleanor and Louis traveled together to the heart of Paris, the Île de la Cité, an oval-shaped island on the Seine River. Enthusiastic crowds, anxious to see their new queen, lined the streets. Linked to the riverbanks by two stone bridges, Eleanor's new home, the Cité Palace, towered above the rooftops. The

This stylized image from 1317 depicts crowded transport along the Seine in Paris, one of the great commercial, governmental, and intellectual centers of medieval Western Europe. *(Courtesy of the Granger Collection.)*

palace was grim and foreboding, with a decaying stone tower with a wide, worn, marble staircase.

Eleanor's small apartments, chiseled out of the rock, were dim and drafty. In one corner was the toilet, consisting of a round seat with a hole that led to a pit below. From the arrow slits that served as windows she could barely glimpse the river below or the evening stars above.

The castle's gardens were more comforting. Surrounded by walls and trellised vines, she could walk down cool paths shaded by willow and fig trees. Roses, lilies, and poppies bloomed in the flowerbeds, and fresh mint scented the air as it twined around pumpkins and leeks. Spreading out from the river was a prosperous, thriving city of nearly 200,000 people. Barges carrying fish and salt traveled the Seine River while men hoisted barrels of wine and sacks of wheat up the steep river-banks. Orchards and small farms flourished on the outskirts of the city.

Paris was a mix of wondrous things, provided people watched where they stepped. Vendors clattered along

A typically bustling and cramped street in medieval Paris. *(Courtesy of the Granger Collection.)*

the noisy, crooked streets, shouting prices for vegetables, fruits, and candles. Merchants circulated, selling waffles, small cakes, and turnovers filled with chopped ham, chicken, and eel.

Paris was the educational center of Europe. Students came from all over the world to study in the city's universities. From Eleanor's garden wall she could see the bridge where the teachers lived. Europe was in the midst of a cultural awakening that had resulted from greater contact with the wider world, particularly the Middle East. During the long period after the collapse of Rome, much of the achievements of the ancient world were lost to Europe. These works had been maintained in Alexandria, Egypt, and other cities around the eastern Mediterranean Sea. There the writings of Aristotle, Plato, Ptolemy, and others had been kept and studied.

Over the preceding decades contact between the east and west had increased, due primarily to the trade and contact that followed the first crusade and Islamic control of Spain. In the twelfth century, European scholars began rediscovering these works, which ignited renewed interest in classical culture and led to the establishment of schools of advanced learning in Paris and other European cities, such as Oxford in England and Padua in Italy. Gradually, education was no longer confined to monasteries, and the subjects studied expanded beyond religion. Scholars often held open-air lectures debating the ideas of classical philosophy. In the summers, the royal gardens in Paris were opened to students, and

Eleanor could listen to debates and lectures in the shade of the fruit trees.

But in general, life in Paris was dull for Eleanor. She had difficulty adjusting to the different attitudes and ways of life. Louis had resumed his religious studies at the cathedral of Notre Dame. He assisted at mass, sang with the cathedral choir, and fasted with the monks on Fridays. His devotion to the Church began to cause friction. Louis refused to participate in Eleanor's merrymaking and spent hours each day in prayer.

As the autumn of 1137 turned to winter, the days became short and dark. Wolves sometimes appeared in the city's narrow, winding streets. Parisians went to bed early, but Eleanor stayed up, shivering in her cold tower room and making plans to improve the palace. At Eleanor's prompting, Louis ordered his wife's room to be modernized. The arrow slits were enlarged to windows and covered with wooden shutters. A chimney and fireplace were built into the wall, and Eleanor ordered tapestries to give her room color and warmth.

Eleanor also reorganized court life at the Cité Palace. The castle smelled like a zoo because it was cluttered with dogs and parrots, few of them housebroken. Eleanor had servants change the rushes, or reeds, covering the floor more often. She also demanded that servants wash their hands before serving food, and set the long tables with tablecloths and napkins.

Eleanor tried to recreate the ambience of her childhood court. She commissioned plays in Latin and

Although Eleanor was described by many in writing, no likenesses exist that were made during her lifetime. This nineteenth-century imagining of the queen takes into account her oft-mentioned lively coloring, lush hair, and unforgettable eyes. *(Courtesy of the Granger Collection.)*

encouraged troubadours to visit and entertain guests, bringing the ideas of courtly love and chivalrous behavior to Paris. As Eleanor helped to popularize the troubadours, she was also scandalizing the Church and northern France, who saw courtly love as merely an excuse for adultery.

Eleanor also brought the fashions of her youth to Paris. Her women wore elaborate headdresses and her men sported curled beards. She loved frivolous, elegant clothes and jewelry. Women in the French court began to mimic her style, wearing fur cloaks and fine wool and silk gowns embroidered with gold thread. Often the cloth was snipped out in circles to show the material beneath. They loaded their arms with jeweled bracelets and wore long, dangling earrings and shoes with pointed toes.

Louis soon fell deeply in love with his new wife, so different from him. He bought Eleanor extravagant gifts from the Orient. "He loved the Queen almost beyond reason," wrote John of Salisbury, one of the pope's secretaries.

Louis's public demonstration of his love for Eleanor made several at court nervous. The queen of France had functions to perform that extended well beyond warming the heart of her husband. She was expected to play an emblematic role in public and to not embarrass the monarchy. But above all she was supposed to produce male heirs. Under French law, only a male could inherit the throne.

Entitled *The Garden of Pleasure,* this Flemish painting depicts a scene of courtly love, reading, and singing, much like what we might imagine from the court that Eleanor strove to create. *(British Library, London)*

The queen's life was tightly circumscribed. Eleanor's days were filled with rounds of prayers and triviality. She and her ladies were expected to sit in the garden on pleasant days, not go hawking as she had in Aquitaine. In bad weather, Eleanor was confined to her apartments, playing chess, singing, telling stories, or chatting. It was a suffocating existence for a girl of intelligence and spirit. When she tried to indulge her own tastes, Louis's shocked courtiers grumbled about the size and cost of Eleanor's household.

Eleanor was the subject of much gossip. "Fie on a beauty that is put on in the morning and laid aside at night!" said Bernard de Clairvaux, who had counseled Eleanor's father but now condemned Eleanor herself. Louis's mother, the former Queen Adelaide, also disapproved of Eleanor. She unleashed a flurry of complaints about Eleanor's makeup and expensive tastes in clothes. She recommended Eleanor pray more and sing less. But Eleanor refused to be relegated to the sidelines. She continued to manage the household and surround herself with her favorite entourage of knights, elegant ladies, and musicians. Despairing, Adelaide retired to her estate.

Criticism of Eleanor was not limited to the royal family. Abbot Suger, who had been Louis's teacher and an adviser to his father, held a powerful sway over Louis and deeply disapproved of Eleanor. Suger was the first person Louis turned to for advice. He had been born poor and had risen to his powerful position through the Church. He had dedicated his life to supporting, maintaining, and expanding the power of the French king. He combined a shrewd intelligence, a careful, conservative manner, and deep religious piety to exert influence on both Louis and the court.

Suger was leery of Eleanor from the start. He distrusted her beauty, her headstrong nature, and her southern origins—and apparently suspected her morals. He also thought that Louis was too immature to rule wisely and was determined to be his primary adviser. Eleanor thought she should have her place of influence, particularly in matters concerning Aquitaine. She and Suger were destined to clash.

Fortunately, there were few external threats at first. Suger's main concern was the tension within France as the noblemen struggled to consolidate their land, power, and wealth. Louis was kind but naïve, once even commenting that he was completely free from enemies.

A challenge soon presented itself. Louis's first test as king was a rebellion in Eleanor's native Poitiers. After Eleanor left home, Louis had installed administrators in key positions. Eleanor's independent subjects resented Louis's rule. They rebelled and declared themselves a commune, not owing allegiance to any overlord.

Louis threw together an army and he and his knights sped to Poitiers, where they caught the rebels off guard and captured the city without a casualty. Louis then made a terrible mistake. He hacked off the rebel leaders' hands, disbanded the commune, and demanded that the rebels' children return with him to Paris as hostages to ensure their fathers' good behavior.

The outcry against Louis's cruelty reached Suger in Paris. He hurried to reason with Louis and arrived at a scene of anguished parents and wailing children. Suger convinced Louis to change his order, but the damage was done. Louis's appalling lack of judgment aroused hatred

Abbot Suger was a respected ecclesiastic, historian, and adviser to Louis VII and his father. *(St. Denis Basilica, Paris)*

and fear throughout southern France, along with Eleanor's disgust. While Louis continued to adore his determined, confident wife, she was annoyed by his immaturity and by his reliance on Abbot Suger instead of her during the entire operation. After all, she knew her lands best.

In the battle between the abbot and the queen, Suger had the advantage. The French monarchy was too institutionally weak for the king to risk alienating such an influential adviser. Suger took steps to curb Eleanor's influence over Louis. While previous French queens had shared in executive decision-making, Suger continuously worked to undercut Eleanor's influence and to deny her any official political power. For the next decade, Eleanor would have a largely ceremonial role despite her intelligence and political aptitude. The powerful French nobility, who feared her influence and maintained a prejudice against southerners, especially southern women, conspired against her. Her sister, Petronilla, was her only reliable ally at court.

Eleanor's first year of disappointment in Paris culminated on Christmas Day in 1137, when she was crowned queen in the city of Bourges in central France. Louis had been crowned by the pope before he married Eleanor. It was a French tradition for the king's heir to be crowned during his father's lifetime. Now, as Eleanor stood inside the domed cathedral of St. Etienne, the air filled with the aroma of incense, the royal crown was placed on her head and she was anointed with sacred oil. Officially becoming queen did little to lift the gloom that seemed to hang over her life in Paris. The following year she had a miscarriage; there was still no heir to the French throne.

Eleanor turned to political intrigue to fill her time. She and Louis hatched a scheme. Without consulting Suger, they decided to claim the county of Toulouse in southern France. Eleanor believed she had a rightful claim to the territory because her grandmother, Philippa, was from Toulouse. Louis agreed; while extending French territory to the Mediterranean Sea, annexing Toulouse would also earn the respect of the other leaders in Europe, as well as his wife. But the king and queen failed to consult their vassals, who were supposed to assist the king during conflicts by providing armor, horses, and men. Several vassals, such as Count Theobald of Champagne, disagreed with Louis's plans and sent nothing.

Louis intended to take Toulouse by surprise, but his haphazard army was undisciplined and ineptly led. The ruler of Toulouse put up strong defenses and Louis had to beat a hasty retreat back to Poitiers, where Eleanor was waiting.

After the embarrassment at Toulouse, Eleanor and Louis lingered in Poitou. They traveled the trails Eleanor remembered from her childhood. During this summer, Eleanor's sister and inseparable companion, Petronilla, began an affair that would dramatically change both of their lives.

Petronilla was a desirable bride. Louis had given her estates in Burgundy and Normandy for her dowry, and she was also the queen's sister. At age nineteen, she had already turned down several marriage proposals before falling in love with Count Raoul of Vermandois. The count, thirty-five years older than Petronilla, was married to the sister of Count Theobald of Champagne. Eleanor urged Raoul to annul his marriage and marry Petronilla. She wanted her sister to be happy, and also to strike a blow at Count Theobald, who had repeatedly failed to honor his feudal obligations.

Before he could marry Petronilla, Raoul's marriage would have to be annulled. Three bishops had to agree to terminate the marriage. Eleanor convinced Louis to round up the three bishops, and early in 1142 Petronilla and Raoul were married. The angry Count Theobald took in his sister and her children and protested the annulment to the pope. Theobald enlisted the help of other prominent nobles, who were eager to drive a wedge between the king and the Church. The pope responded by excommunicating the three bishops and ordering Raoul to return to his wife. When Raoul refused, he and Petronilla were also excommunicated.

Louis considered the pope's actions to be an attack on his authority. Blaming Theobald, Louis plotted his revenge. He sent his army to Theobald's lands, where they burned villages, ravaged fields, and left dozens of corpses behind. Stubbornly, the count stood his ground.

In January of 1143, Louis laid siege to the small town of Vitry-sur-Marne in northeastern France. The village clustered around one of Count Theobald's castles, which Louis aimed to occupy. When the king and his army arrived, the local people were terrified and sought shelter within the town's walls. From a nearby hill, Louis watched as his men attacked the wooden castle and houses with flaming arrows. Soon the town was ablaze. Panic-stricken, more than one thousand people fled to the safety of the village's stone cathedral. But wind spread the fire and soon flames licked at the cathedral's wooden roof. When the roof collapsed, everyone inside died.

From his hill, Louis heard the townspeople's screams. Horrified, he was unable to speak. At night he wept into his pillows, blaming himself, and suffered terrible nightmares. The town was renamed Vitry-le-Brûlé, or

"Vitry-the-Burned." The tide of public opinion turned against Louis and Eleanor. Bernard de Clairvaux sent thundering letters to Louis condemning him for his actions: "For from whom except the devil can I say that this counsel proceeds that adds fire to fire and slaughter to slaughter . . ." He believed Eleanor was advising Louis in an effort to wield power and advance her own goals. But Louis was king, and he was the one ultimately held responsible for the war.

Louis broke down emotionally. Wracked with guilt for the lives lost, he spent hours at prayer seeking forgiveness. Like a monk, he shaved his head and wore a coarse gray robe and sandals. The king's melancholy wore off on Eleanor. They had now been married for seven years and she still had not borne a single child. Her principal duty was to produce an heir. This failure became a near obsession, and she sought Bernard de Clairvaux's help. Even though he disapproved of her attire, actions, and behavior, he was an important holy man, and she needed a way to meet with him. She soon found an opportunity.

Abbot Suger decided to beautify the cathedral of St. Denis in Paris. The cathedral was built in the Romanesque style, with massive, thick stone walls and supports called vaults to hold up the domed roofs and arched windows. Suger had radical ideas. Wanting to let more light into the dim cathedral, his stonemasons experimented with cutting-edge construction techniques. They used thin, intersecting arches, called rib vaults, to support the roof, as well as innovative external stone supports called flying buttresses. The cathedral no longer needed thick stone walls to keep it standing. Massive stained-glass windows gave the appearance of walls of glass.

St. Denis was the first true example in Europe of a new type of architecture referred to as Gothic. It launched a period of building elegantly arched cathedrals that rose higher and higher over the years. The cathedrals were topped with gargoyles, stone sculptures of monsters, mythical creatures, and even ugly mothers-in-law. By the end of the twelfth century, Gothic architecture was flourishing.

On June 10, 1144, Eleanor and Louis arrived at a ceremony to unveil St. Denis. A peace conference to mend the conflict in Champagne was scheduled afterwards, with Bernard in attendance. Crowds thronged the roads to see the remodeled cathedral's pointed stone arches and vast stained-glass windows, which bathed the cathedral in shimmering pools of gem-colored light. A twenty-foot-tall gold cross, glittering with diamonds, pearls, and rubies, rose from the altar amidst a haze of incense. The altar was filled with gold, silver, and jeweled vases, donated by French lords, including the wedding vase Eleanor gave to Louis.

Louis dressed like a monk during the ceremony. He carried the container holding St. Denis's bones to the altar. While some people scoffed at his monastic garb, others were impressed by his devotion. "No one would have taken the king for that scourge of war who had lately destroyed

When Abbot Suger undertook the project of redesigning the cathedral of St. Denis, he wanted to create a building with a high degree of linearity that was flushed with light and color. The first truly Gothic construction was the choir of the church, consecrated in 1144. With its thin columns, stained-glass windows, and a sense of verticality with an ethereal look, the choir of St. Denis established the elements that would later be elaborated upon during the Gothic period. *(AP Photo)*

so many towns, burned so many churches, shed so much blood," wrote the monk Gervase of Canterbury.

Eleanor's dress contrasted sharply with her humble husband's. In a silk gown with tight-fitting sleeves, she wore a veil, or wimple, held in place by a pearl and gold crown. Her long earrings, bracelets, and a jeweled belt around her slender waist shimmered as she walked. Over her gown she wore a red velvet robe with wide sleeves that tapered to points, nearly touching the ground.

After the ceremony, Eleanor met with Bernard. Hoping to convince him to help lift the excommunications against Petronilla and Raoul, she offered to persuade Louis to make peace with Theobald. Bernard was horrified at Eleanor's boldness. He had expected pleas for forgiveness, not bargaining, and sharply reprimanded her for meddling in church and state affairs and for being a disobedient wife. Eleanor broke into tears, saying she was bitter because of her failure to have children, and that she dabbled in politics because her life was lonely. She pleaded with Bernard to add his prayers to hers so that she could become a mother. Gratified by Eleanor's apparently sincere wishes to fulfill her womanly duty, Bernard softened. "My child," he said, "seek those things which make for peace. Cease to stir up the king against the Church . . . If you will promise to do this, I in my turn promise to entreat the merciful Lord to grant you offspring."

As dusk fell over the abbey Eleanor hurried off to find Louis. Whether through manipulation or earnest tears, Eleanor's meeting with Bernard had achieved the pact she most desired. Later that day, Louis made concessions, returning Theobald's lands. Eventually, the pope recognized Petronilla and Raoul's marriage, although they remained excommunicated.

Within a year, Eleanor had her first child. She named her tiny daughter Marie, in tribute to the Virgin Mary. Although Marie might inherit Aquitaine, she could never inherit the French throne. Still, there was renewed hope for a son in the future.

Outwardly, peace seemed to have returned. Unlike other countries in Europe, the kingdom of France had few external enemies. The various German territories,

Theologian, abbot, and future saint Bernard de Clairvaux became known for his conservative Christian perspective during Europe's intellectual revival in the twelfth-century. *(Bibliothèque Nationale, Paris)*

without any natural borders dividing them, seemed to reel from one crisis to the next. Their rulers often had tense relations with the pope and the Catholic Church in Rome and were loosely held together under a state called the Holy Roman Empire. It consisted of large parts of present-day Germany as well as parts of Italy, the Netherlands, and Austria. This far-flung empire seemed to always be involved in a dispute.

England, too, was gradually descending into anarchy. King Stephen struggled to hold onto his throne as noblemen took advantage of his weak rule. A rash of private feuds and wars broke out. Marauders from Scotland and Wales committed atrocities during border disputes. Foreign mercenaries kidnapped civilians and held them for ransom. Years of famine added to the misery.

Although their realm was at peace, Eleanor and Louis were not. Louis grew jealous of Eleanor's beauty, charm, and social graces. She was so much more likeable than he. Additionally, the queen had invited the troubadour Marcabru to Paris. He was popular in Aquitaine for his poetic talent; she had known him as a girl and was thrilled when he accepted her invitation. When Marcabru arrived, he wrote passionate verses about his patroness, as was typical, but Louis misread the situation. Although there was no hint that Eleanor and Marcabru had an affair, Louis banished him from court.

Troubled and insecure, Louis still was stricken with grief about the deaths at Vitry. He wore a coarse hair shirt and began to consider making a pilgrimage to Jerusalem to atone for his sins. Eleanor began to seriously regret her marriage to the king of France, but there was little she could do to change the situation.

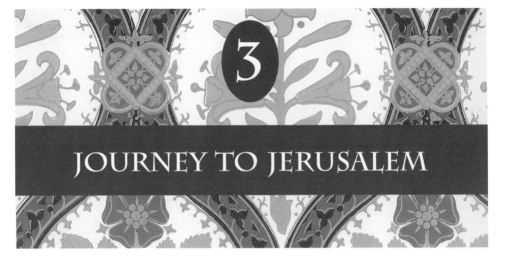

JOURNEY TO JERUSALEM

Just before Christmas in 1145, a messenger arrived at Eleanor and Louis's court with a request that promised an escape from their problems. Pope Eugenius III was asking them to join a crusade to liberate the Holy Lands from Muslim control.

This would be the Second Crusade. The first had begun in 1095, when Pope Urban II had summoned all Christian knights to drive the Islamic Turks out of the Holy Lands and, most importantly, to liberate the city of Jerusalem.

Since the birth of Islam in the seventh century, the Byzantine Empire had been under intense pressure from Islamic fighters. With its capital at Constantinople (present-day Istanbul), the Christian empire was increasingly surrounded by the Turkish-led forces of Islam.

In 1095, Pope Urban II arrived in France at the Council of Clemont to encourage support for the First Crusade. *(Bibliothèque Nationale, Paris)*

In 1071 the Byzantine army suffered a crushing defeat at the Battle of Manzikert. Stories began filtering into the west of Turkish attacks on Christian pilgrims in Jerusalem. When the Byzantine emperor Alexius Comnenus sent envoys to Urban II asking for help, the pope responded with a call for knights to "take up the cross" and liberate the Holy Lands.

The First Crusade succeeded in taking control of Jerusalem and surrounding areas in only three years. The conquered territory was organized into four crusader states—Edessa, Antioch, Tripolis, and the kingdom of Jerusalem, which was supposed to be the overlord of the other crusader states. But the ruler of Jerusalem had little success exerting authority over his neighbors. Ongoing dissension and clashing ambitions among the rulers undermined their power.

The Second Crusade was called because the Muslims had begun to make inroads in recovering territory. When Edessa fell to the Turks in 1144, the pope called for its recapture by a new generation of knights and European rulers.

The pope offered his forgiveness for Louis and Eleanor's sins if they agreed to help to free the Holy Lands from the Turks. When the pope's message reached Paris, Louis was weak from fasting. His sense of unworthiness was deeper than ever. He and Eleanor, for different reasons, leaped at the chance to go fight the Turks. A holy war against infidels offered Louis the chance to atone for his crimes at Vitry and to restore his international prestige. Eleanor saw it as an opportunity for adventure and a welcome escape from her boring court routine.

On Christmas Day 1145, the king and queen announced their plan to lead the Second Crusade. Many people received the idea coldly. Some thought Louis was thinking more of his own penance than of service to Christianity. Others remembered his prior military campaigns, which had ended in disaster. Suger urged Eleanor and Louis to reconsider. Louis had no heir; if he should die, the realm would be thrown into turmoil. Despite the Truce of God, a papal decree forbidding the invasion of a crusader's lands during his service to the Church, France would be unstable with the king and queen gone. Eleanor's vassals were also lukewarm. They remembered Eleanor's grandfather's journey to the Holy Lands, where 70,000 of their countrymen had died.

Eleanor and Louis were asking their subjects to face danger and possible death on a perilous, yearlong journey that would culminate in violent battle.

Organizing the crusade was difficult. By Easter of 1146 more volunteers were still needed. Bernard preached to a huge crowd in a field in eastern France. Eleanor and Louis were present when Bernard vowed

Bernard de Clairvaux preaches the Second Crusade in the presence of King Louis VII. *(Courtesy of Art Resource.)*

that those who took the cross would be forgiven their sins and would receive everlasting rewards. He pinned a red cross, the symbol of the crusade, on Louis's tunic as the king wept. After hearing Bernard's sermon, people rushed forward to enlist and to receive their red crosses. Nobles shouted, "Crosses, crosses, give us crosses!" As the sun sank and the valley filled with mist, Bernard ran out of crosses. Amidst cries of "To Jerusalem!" he flung off his wool cloak and began snipping it into little crosses. Religious furor for the crusade had hit a fevered pitch. "I opened my mouth and I spoke and the crusaders at once multiplied into infinity," Bernard wrote to the pope. "Villages and towns are deserted and you will scarcely find one man for every seven women. Everywhere you will see widows whose husbands are still alive."

Other women followed Eleanor's example. At least three hundred women volunteered to come along to nurse the wounded, a brave decision; many of the Christian women on the First Crusade had died or been sold as slaves. After receiving their crosses, Eleanor and her ladies dressed themselves as warriors in white tunics with red crosses and cherry-red boots. They galloped on white horses through the crowds, calling people to heed God's summons.

The crusaders had various motivations. Some saw the crusade as a religious duty; others jumped at the chance for excitement and the adventure of travel to faraway places. The appeal of land and plunder drew a great many. Many of the veterans of the first crusade had lingered in the east and set up feudal territories of their own.

Eleanor toured her domains whipping up support. She played on people's pride, encouraged their ambition, and chastised their cowardliness. She also raised money by organizing town fairs and tournaments with entrance fees. Soon Eleanor's vassals comprised a large part of the crusading army. Aquitanian and French nobles put aside their differences and united; Europe was again aflame with crusading fervor. Eleanor also gathered minstrels and troubadours for the crusade, although they had been forbidden as distractions by Bernard.

Planning and organizing for the crusade required a staggering amount of work. They needed food for 100,000 people for a journey of more than 3,000 miles, as well as transportation and guides to lead them through strange and sometimes hostile lands.

It would also be an expensive undertaking. Eleanor's baggage alone filled a line of wagons. She and her ladies took jewelry, cosmetics, silk gowns, belts, furs, tents, carpets, soaps, goblets, and washbasins. She was criticized for packing so heavily. Louis imposed heavy taxes to raise money, and churches donated their treasures.

On June 8, 1147, by the light of one thousand candles in the cathedral of St. Denis, Louis placed his kingdom in Suger's hands. Dressed in a black tunic with a red cross, Louis received the Oriflamme, or flag of France, from the pope to take to the Holy Lands. Like Louis, Eleanor wept with emotion.

Church bells pealed and crowds cheered as the

Louis's undertaking of the Second Crusade is glorified in this stained-glass panel from the twelfth-century cathedral at Senlis. *(Senlis Cathedral)*

crusaders said their farewells. People leaned from windows and sat on rooftops to watch the parade of archers with longbows, noble ladies dressed as brilliantly as peacocks, minstrels, wagons, packs of hunting dogs, and pet monkeys. The ladies carried falcons on their wrists, as if going on a hunting party. Many of the men carried swords with splinters believed to be from Jesus' cross set into the hilts. "Anyone seeing these cohorts with their helmets and buckles shining in the sun, with their banners streaming in the breeze, would have been certain that they were about to triumph over all the enemies of the cross and reduce to submission all the countries of the Orient," wrote one chronicler.

In robes embroidered with white lilies, Eleanor sat

proudly and gracefully in her silver saddle, her horse's mane braided for the occasion. She was leaving the constraints of her ordinary life as well as her two-year-old daughter, Marie, behind. As royal parents, Eleanor and Louis were busy and often absent from Marie's daily life. Their tiny daughter had her own household.

The crusade, at its outset, was like a grand party going on a glorious sightseeing tour. To the tune of thumping hooves and creaking wagon wheels, people sang hymns and marching songs. There was an instant camaraderie between Eleanor and the Aquitainians. All day long, Eleanor could converse in her native tongue, just like during her childhood.

The crusaders took a land route to Constantinople. They awoke before dawn, dressed, and prayed. Then they dismantled their tents, harnessed their carts, and began traveling. If any wild birds were spotted overhead, the ladies released their falcons. When the women blew a whistle, their well-trained falcons brought back the prey for dinner. In the late afternoon, after traveling between ten and twenty miles, the crusaders stopped, lit fires, and drew baths for the women.

Inevitably, a social rift developed between the northerners, who had often disapproved of their king's wife, and Eleanor and her southern compatriots. Rumors spread that the queen was not being entirely faithful to her husband. Louis was caught in the middle, not wanting to antagonize Eleanor's vassals, who made up the bulk of his army, but angry at Eleanor and jealous of her ease and beauty.

As they traveled, Louis expected his soldiers to behave in a godly manner, but his authority was unraveling. The crusaders' food began to run out and they started to pillage the farms and villages along their route. They even murdered one merchant who protested when the crusaders stole food. Odo de Deuil, Louis's secretary writing the official story of their travels, commented it would be a waste of time to list Louis's rules, as not one was followed. Worried by Louis's mismanagement of the food supply and his inability to impose discipline, people began to desert.

The crusaders crossed into Greece behind a larger force of German fighters who were pillaging and murdering across Asia Minor. The French crusaders found the route dotted with dead German stragglers killed by angry Greeks. Eleanor and her ladies wrapped their veils over their faces to keep out the smell and grimly rode on. Now the crusade was becoming a test of endurance, as skirmishes arose between the Greeks and the hungry, out-of-control crusaders. The French were relieved when they finally arrived in Constantinople, where they hoped to find plenty of food. As they entered the exotic city of Constantinople, Louis wrote to Suger, "The Lord is aiding us at every turn." He spoke too soon.

Constantinople had been founded to govern the eastern part of the Roman Empire. After the collapse of Rome, it had become the capital of the Byzantine

This image from a fifteenth-century illuminated manuscript depicts the entrance of Louis VII *(center, in blue)* and his army into Constantinople during the Second Crusade. He is joined by the German king Conrad III *(left, in gold)*. *(Courtesy of Art Resource.)*

Empire. Although the Byzantine Empire was Christian, it had developed its own traditions in religion, politics, and culture. Religion in Byzantium was governed by the Eastern Orthodox Church, which for centuries had maintained a tense relationship with the Roman Catholic Church.

It was said that the Orthodox Church possessed two-thirds of the world's wealth and more than four thousand palaces, churches, and convents. Eleanor passed shops selling colorful Chinese and Indian silks, gleaming precious jewels, and Russian furs. She walked on tiled paths through beautiful gardens and on soft Persian carpets. Hosted by the Byzantine emperor, Manuel Comnenus, she and Louis feasted on rare delicacies such as artichokes, caviar, and sauces cooked with exotic spices such as cinnamon, pepper, and sugar. They drank chilled wine from glasses and ate with forks, which were not yet common in the West. The emperor organized hunting expeditions with tame leopards and showed his visitors the town's sacred relics, which were believed to be from Jesus: a crown of thorns and a nail from the cross.

Louis hoped Comnenus would aid him, but the emperor had his own problems. Comnenus was being threatened on all sides. For years, his lands had been attacked by the Turks. He was also on the brink of war with King Roger of Sicily, who had unified many small states in southern Italy and conquered parts of North Africa. Not wanting war with the Turks and the Sicilians at the same time, Comnenus had recently concluded a truce with the Turks. If he assisted the European crusaders it would anger the Turks. For Comnenus, the best solution was for the Turks and the crusaders to destroy each other. While Louis and his mob-like army lingered in Constantinople, Emperor Comnenus was hoping to hurry them on to their destruction.

It did not take long for Louis's army to wear out its welcome. When his soldiers drunkenly terrorized Constantinople, Louis initially did little to stop them. When it became evident he had to do something he sent Eleanor and the army ahead to the coast of Asia Minor. Then Louis approached Comnenus for a last-minute conference. The emperor, dismayed to see Louis return, told him that the German army had won a great victory and killed 14,000 Turks. Actually, the Turks had recently slaughtered ninety percent of the German fighters. The unsuspecting Louis hurried to rejoin his army.

A few days later the French army came across the remains of the German fighters, and Louis finally realized that Comnenus had betrayed him. The Turks were lying in wait for the French. Nervous that they were about to be ambushed by the Turks, they traveled south through Asia Minor. Their horses began dying from starvation and the crusaders sold their shields, helmets, and gowns for food. More supplies were lost in a flood. It had been seven months since the crusade began and they did not know where they were or how to proceed. Louis had divided the leadership between his nobles, which meant there was no strong leader when one was needed. But they pressed on, harassed daily by Turkish raiding parties on fast ponies. Eleanor and the ladies traveled in horse-drawn litters with closed leather curtains. At night, they sheltered under the remaining tents.

In January of 1148, disaster struck in the mountains of Paphlagonia in western Asia Minor. Louis sent Eleanor ahead with part of the army to set up camp on a plateau before the next mountain pass. Instead of stopping at the windswept plateau, they continued on to a sheltered valley. When the main army reached the plateau, Louis sent scouts ahead to find Eleanor. As the army waited by the rocky pass, the Turks swooped down upon them and slaughtered nearly 7,000 crusaders. Louis barely escaped with his life.

At midnight, a search party from Eleanor's camp met the exhausted survivors. Looking for a scapegoat for the tragedy, the northerners blamed Eleanor and the Aquitainians that had escaped disaster by remaining with her. They believed Eleanor had caused the tragedy by disobeying Louis's orders and by spreading the army too thin. But it was Louis who had failed to maintain order and discipline.

The glorious adventure had turned into a nightmare. The Turks continued to harass the crusaders, who were forced to eat their dead horses and drink animal blood to survive. Everyone's hands were raw and blistered, their lips were cracked, and their clothes were filthy rags. Winter storms with strong winds hounded them.

The crusaders reached Attalia in southern Asia Minor on the coast of the Mediterranean Sea and decided to finish the journey by sea. Nearly 7,000 who could not afford the boat fare were left behind. Many of them starved, died of the plague, or became Muslims, enticed by food from the Turks. The crusaders who could afford to pay their way reached Antioch, in northern Syria, three weeks later.

Antioch reminded Eleanor of her hometown of Poitiers with its tropical plants and rivers full of ships. Antioch was the crossroads of traffic for silks and spices from the Orient and ivory and grains from Egypt. A mix of eastern and western cultures, it was a prosperous city.

The city's ruler was Eleanor's uncle Raymond. He threw an exquisite banquet, where they dined on oranges, melons, apples of paradise, bananas, and the choice dish of lettuce. Eleanor had known Raymond since she was a child and they spent much time together. He presented her with costly gifts of silken gowns and perfumes. Louis began to grow jealous of the easy way they enjoyed each other's company, their intimate laughter, and the indecipherable jokes they shared in langue d'oc. He imagined his wife was flirting with her uncle. "His constant, indeed almost continuous conversation with her aroused the King's suspicions," said John of Salisbury, an English philosopher and historian.

Eleanor and Louis began to argue. Adding fuel to the fire, Eleanor supported Raymond's tactical suggestions for the crusaders; they thought the crusaders should recapture Edessa and reinforce Antioch against the Turks. Antioch would then provide a buffer between the Turks and Jerusalem. Louis disagreed. He wanted to head straight for Jerusalem.

As Eleanor and Raymond joined forces against Louis, rumors circulated. Many people, Louis included, thought she was having an affair with Raymond. In a loud, public argument, Eleanor declared that if Louis did not attack Edessa, she and her vassals would remain in Antioch, paralyzing the crusaders' chances of success. A surprised Louis threatened to tear her away from Antioch, as was his right as her husband.

While women in the twelfth century might sometimes

This nineteenth-century image depicts Queen Eleanor with her entourage of troubadours in Antioch, Syria, during the Second Crusade. *(Courtesy of the Granger Collection.)*

have disagreed with their husbands, few acted upon their feelings. They often accepted an unhappy marriage, either for financial reasons or because they believed their husbands were their masters. Usually when a marriage ended it was the man's decision, and the woman silently returned to her father's castle or entered a convent. Not Eleanor. For her, life with Louis had reached an unendurable point. A dull husband might be tolerable, but she could not live with a fool. She was convinced that thousands had died on the crusade because of his foolishness.

Eleanor told Louis she wanted to annul their marriage. She thought the fact they were distant cousins was sufficient grounds to get the pope's approval. Eleanor even suggested she had been unable to have sons because God was displeased with their marriage. She suggested that Louis return to France and she remain in Antioch while the annulment was arranged.

Louis was hurt and angry at the suggestion. He probably still loved his wife, but more than anything he did not want to lose control of her lands. He confided his feelings to his bodyguard, Thierry Galan, who disliked Eleanor. Galan suggested Louis force Eleanor to accompany him to Jerusalem. "It would be a lasting shame to the kingdom of the Franks if in addition to all the other disasters it was reported that the king had been deserted by his wife, or robbed of her," he said.

On March 28, Louis gave orders for Eleanor to be arrested. She was seized at midnight and taken to the king, who was with his army outside of Antioch. Eleanor never had the chance to say goodbye to her uncle, who would soon be killed in a skirmish with the Turks.

Suddenly Eleanor was on the road to Jerusalem, by Louis's side. They passed groves of orange trees and thick flocks of sheep as they wound over mountains high above the Mediterranean Sea. She was heavily guarded; there was little chance for escape. By disgracing her in this way, Louis had only widened the division between them. "Their mutual anger growing greater, the wound remained, hide it as best they might," wrote John of Salisbury.

In May of 1148, the bedraggled crusaders reached Jerusalem. They fell to their knees and wept. Louis and Eleanor, who was still kept under discreet watch, toured the city.

Jerusalem was in no danger of imminent attack, which meant that Raymond's plan to drive the Turks north before they attacked Antioch had made sense. But Louis insisted Jerusalem needed to be defended. Wanting to present some achievement to Christendom to prove his skill and religious devotion, Louis met with local leaders to develop a plan.

Louis was persuaded to attack Damascus, which turned into an immense blunder. The siege lasted four days, after which the crusaders retreated. The defeat marked the end of the crusade. Thousands of lives had been lost without any territorial gain. Dogged by disaster, and drained of money and morale, the French army melted away. In France, the news was met with sadness and anger.

After the defeat Eleanor expected to leave Jerusalem any day, but Louis dawdled. He spent most of his time praying and visiting holy sites. They stayed in Jerusalem until the following Easter; obviously, the king was not anxious to return to France after his unsuccessful crusade.

When Eleanor and Louis finally left Jerusalem, they boarded separate ships bound for Sicily. Eleanor's ship was blown off course and delayed for two months. When she landed in Italy, exhausted and weak, Eleanor joined Louis in Rome, where they stayed with the pope. There she expressed her doubts about the validity of her marriage. The pope listened to her concerns, but he refused to annul the marriage and even insisted that the couple sleep together in a bed he had draped with silk hangings.

On November 11, 1149, after a two-year absence, Eleanor and Louis returned to Paris. The crusaders who trickled home before them had told tales of disaster and woe. Even Odo de Deuil had stopped writing about the crusade because there was nothing good to say. Louis, he said, "was not able to do anything useful, anything worthy of mention, or actually anything worthy of France." Eleanor was unpopular, too. Devout Christians pondered the failures. "It remains a mystery to the feeble judgment of mankind why Our Lord should suffer the French, who of all the people in the world have the deepest faith and most honour Him, to be destroyed by the enemies of religion," commented William of Tyre.

The Second Crusade did help to open trade routes between Europe and the Far East. Eleanor brought back roses, mulberry trees, and silkworms to France. The twenty-eight-year-old queen also returned with a secret. She was pregnant.

In the second half of 1150, Eleanor had another daughter, Alix. Although Eleanor knew Louis wanted a son, she was happy. Her second daughter might be the key to escaping her marriage. She had failed again to produce an heir to the French throne. Eleanor's once-private struggle for divorce now became a matter for Louis's council, who voiced concerns that Eleanor might only have daughters. They urged Louis to have his marriage annulled and marry a woman who could give him sons.

The need for an heir was the overwhelming concern, but the couple was clearly unhappy. As the year ended, bitter weather fell over Paris. Roads were impassable and rivers iced over. Inside the freezing Cité Palace, Louis and Eleanor argued. Louis had cut his hair like a priest and was spending even longer hours in prayer to atone for his failed crusade. Eleanor lamented that she had married a monk instead of a king.

Suger argued against the divorce for several reasons. For one, Eleanor and Louis could have more children. Aquitaine was also a rich property for Louis to lose. If Eleanor remarried, her lands could fall into enemy hands; Suger wanted Eleanor's lands to remain in the French domain, despite the king's inability to manage them.

This final obstacle against the annulment disappeared when Suger died in the winter following Alix's birth. Without Suger's opposition, the thought of leaving a marriage with which God was seemingly displeased, and the allure of having a son and heir, began to appeal to Louis.

But first Louis needed to resolve a dispute with two of his vassals, Geoffrey of Anjou and his son Henry. The Anjou family was nicknamed Plantagenet because Geoffrey's father had worn a flower called a *Planta genista* on his hat. In 1141, Geoffrey had conquered Normandy, a large territory in the northwest of present-day France, and had named his son Henry the duke of Normandy. But Henry did not want to pay homage to Louis as his overlord, and Louis refused to recognize him as duke.

Louis summoned both father and son to Paris to pay homage to him and to answer charges

Geoffrey of Anjou. *(Musée de Tessé, Le Mans)*

that Geoffrey had captured one of the king's officials in a land dispute. The Plantagenets showed up for their audience with the king holding Louis's officer in chains. Bernard de Clairvaux, who was helping to mediate the dispute, demanded they release the prisoner. Geoffrey flew into a rage and stalked away as the monk thundered that Geoffrey would meet an early death. Despite this inauspicious beginning, Geoffrey and Henry stayed in Paris for a week. When they returned to the castle a few days after their first meeting, they offered Louis the Vexin, a small strip of land on the border of Normandy and France, in return for recognizing Henry as duke. Geoffrey also agreed to release the king's official. Geoffrey's sudden turnaround baffled Louis. As the days passed Geoffrey began to seriously fret over Bernard's grave prediction.

Eleanor was drawn to Geoffrey's stocky, restless, eighteen-year-old son. Although Eleanor was ten years older, Henry was equally attracted to her. No doubt Henry also found it attractive that the elegant and so-phisticated Eleanor controlled most of the land between the Loire River and the Pyrenees Mountains. Some even speculated that the savvy queen and the young duke had made secret plans to marry and thus build a dynasty that would cover much of western France.

After their cordial meeting with Louis, Geoffrey and Henry left for Normandy. It would not be long before Henry and Eleanor had the opportunity to set their supposed plans in motion.

4

A New Life

On March 21, 1152, Pope Eugenius granted Eleanor and Louis's request for an annulment. Eleanor's two daughters, Marie and Alix, were placed in Louis's care.

During Eleanor's lifetime, it was widely believed that Louis had divorced her for adultery, but out of kindness to her reputation agreed to conceal his motives. Louis's real motive was the need to produce an heir. This outweighed even the importance of retaining nominal control of Eleanor's ungovernable lands.

The annulment ceremony was held near the city of Orléans in March. When it was over and she was an unmarried woman, Eleanor left Louis for the last time. They would never meet again.

On a warm day in late March, Eleanor took the road to Poitiers as a free woman. She had spent years waiting for pregnancies, waiting to depart for the crusade, waiting to leave the Holy Lands, and waiting to be free of Louis. Despite her forced subservience, she had never stopped trying to find an independent role. Pleasure in life for Eleanor meant political and personal independence. It would remain an elusive goal.

As she traveled south, people lined up to wave and stare at her. It was not a carefree journey. Despite her escort, Eleanor was in a dangerous position. As the single female ruler of a wealthy territory, she attracted fortune hunters. One of those fortune hunters lurked just outside of Paris. Theobald of Blois, future count of the territory of Blois west of Louis's kingdom, planned to abduct Eleanor and marry her. Eleanor avoided him by fleeing on a barge down the Loire River at night. Closer to Poitiers, Count Geoffrey of Nantes, Henry Plantagent's younger brother, was lying in wait; as second son, Geoffrey would inherit little, if any, of his father's territory. Warned of his plans, Eleanor changed her route and narrowly avoided his clutches.

Once safely back in Poitiers, Eleanor enjoyed her freedom. Anxious to rid Aquitaine of Louis's influence, she rescinded all of his laws. She issued documents in her own name and summoned her vassals to renew their allegiance to her.

Eleanor's unmarried status would not last long. Unless she wanted to be constantly surrounded by bodyguards, life without a powerful husband would be perilous. If she did not marry someone of her own choosing soon, she might not have any choice in the matter. Eleanor sent a message to Henry.

Much had changed in Henry's life. True to Bernard's predictions, his father had died shortly after the meeting in Paris. Henry was now the head of the Anjou family, which comprised the Angevin dynasty. Hot-tempered and energetic, the Anjous were skilled at war and notorious for their family feuds, sexual appetites, and thirst for land and power. A family legend told of an ancestor who had married Satan's daughter. She bore his children and then returned to Hell. The family joked they were descended directly from the devil.

The oldest of three sons, Henry was born on March 5, 1133. Handsome, with reddish-gold hair, a freckled face, and gray eyes, Henry was also well educated, highly intelligent, and could speak Latin and French. Hardworking and intense, he had a spectacular temper. "At crack of dawn he was off on horseback," wrote Gerald of Wales, a clergyman and medieval chronicler, "traversing wastelands, penetrating forests and climbing the mountaintops. . . . At evening, on his return home, he was rarely seen to sit down, either before or after supper. And despite such tremendous exertions, he would wear out the whole court by remaining on his feet."

Marriage made political sense for both Henry and Eleanor. Henry had the strength and vigor to govern her unruly vassals. By marrying Eleanor, Henry would double his territories, including strategic cities and castles, and establish himself as a powerful force in Europe. But the

Eleanor's second husband, Henry of Anjou, later Henry II of England. (Cassell's History of England, *1902)*

marriage was a gamble. Aquitaine would be difficult to govern, as the people resented outsiders, and he did not know if Eleanor could have sons. But these were risks he was willing to take.

Henry's main preoccupation was his claim to the throne of England. His mother, Matilda, was the sole heiress of her father, King Henry I of England. Upon her father's death in 1135, her cousin Stephen was crowned instead. The English nobles had wanted a male ruler. Matilda had launched a war to claim her throne. She was ultimately driven out of the country and forced to escape, camouflaged in a white cloak during a blizzard. Matilda was still called "empress" because she had been married to a German emperor before marrying Henry's father. After Geoffrey's death she relinquished her claim to the English throne to her son and retired to the city of Rouen in Normandy.

As Henry Plantagenet arrived on Eleanor's doorstep, she knew they shared cultural and political interests, energy, and ambition. Together they could accomplish much.

On May 18, 1152, Eleanor and Henry were married in a simple ceremony in the cathedral of Poitiers. Witnessed only by family and close friends, their marriage was nevertheless daring. Louis was their overlord and they were supposed to request his permission to marry, but they knew he would never grant it. Henry's plans to unite Normandy, Anjou, Aquitaine, and England would isolate France. Eleanor and Henry were forging an empire that would change the face of Europe.

News of Eleanor's hasty remarriage shocked the rulers of Europe. Louis was the hardest hit. For Eleanor to remarry so soon was not only a personal insult, but also a political threat. Henry was his biggest rival.

Eleanor's separation from Louis had already damaged her reputation; her new marriage further fanned the gossip about her alleged affairs and unconventional behavior. Louis formed a group of those disgruntled by Eleanor's marriage. Eleanor's two would-be ambushers, Louis's brother, and the king of England's son, Eustace, were part of the coalition. They charged into Normandy to confront Henry.

Within six weeks Henry routed each of his opponents. He rode so quickly between them that his horses collapsed from exhaustion. Louis, now ill, retreated home and pondered his losses. Henry had triumphantly established himself as a dominant power in Western Europe and now he returned to his new wife.

Eleanor and Henry decided to make a progress through Eleanor's lands. They met with old friends and sipped garnet-colored wines. During the days, Eleanor loosed her falcons in the deep blue autumn skies. At night, she reveled in banquet halls blazing with candles and filled with song and laughter.

Although Eleanor was popular, her vassals feared Henry would squeeze money from them in order to pay for his war in England. When they pitched their tents outside the walls of one city, Henry and Eleanor received a kind welcome, but at mealtime their cook complained the town had not sent out any food. The town retorted they were only required to feed Eleanor and her husband when they lodged within city walls. This insult infuriated Henry. He threw himself to the ground, kicking and screaming; he bit blankets and smashed furniture. When his tantrum ended, he destroyed the walls of the city to keep such an insult from happening again. Despite Henry's sometimes erratic behavior, southern France still adored Eleanor, and she was happy with her new marriage.

As the year ended, Henry traveled to Normandy to prepare for his invasion of England. He left Eleanor ruling Anjou and Aquitaine, and his mother, Matilda, governing Normandy. He also left with the announcement that Eleanor was pregnant.

After a stormy crossing, Henry landed on the southern coast of England in January of 1153. Everything conspired in his favor, even the weather, as he launched his attack on King Stephen. "The floodgates of heaven were opened and heavy rain drove in the faces of Stephen's men, with violent gusts of wind and severe cold, so that God himself appeared to fight for the duke," recorded medieval writer Henry of Huntingdon.

Henry's reputation for bravery and military skill had preceded him. The war-weary nobles of England began to support him with money and troops. They were sick of the civil war and chaos under Stephen's reign. Eager for peace, they pressed Stephen to acknowledge Henry as his heir.

Back in Aquitaine, Eleanor worked to reestablish the civilized court of her childhood. She wanted her court to be a place where music, poetry, and literature flourished. Her court became a magnet for wandering minstrels and poets, who sang her praises. One troubadour, Bernard de Ventadour, wrote romantic songs expressing

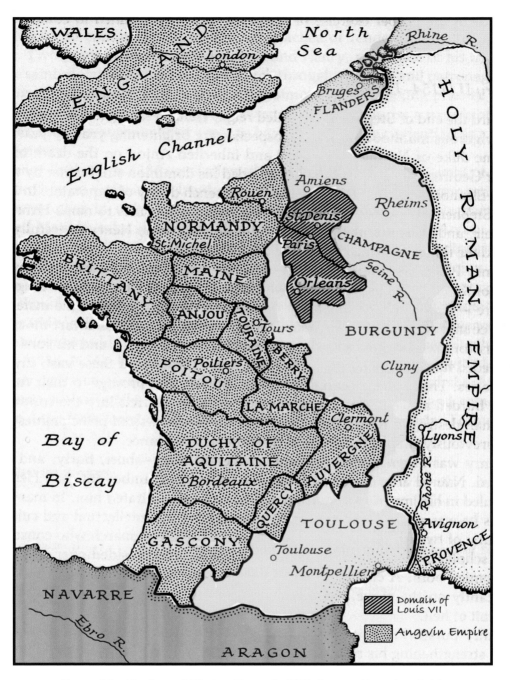

Some of the kingdoms of Western Europe in 1154, the year Henry traveled to England to claim his throne.

the ideals of chivalry and love Eleanor was so eager to spread. Delighted she could read, Bernard wrote poems containing secret messages for her eyes alone. Inspired, he fell in love with her. "You have been the first among my joys and you shall be the last, so long as there is life in me," Bernard wrote to Eleanor.

Eleanor enjoyed the flattery, even expecting and encouraging such courtly games. But when word of the flirtations reached Henry back in England, he was less than thrilled. Unfamiliar with the culture and games of courtly love, he was alarmed at Eleanor's relationship with her troubadour. He summoned Bernard to England to write songs for the war. A miserable Bernard left Aquitaine, although he would never forget Eleanor. He described himself as "a man beyond hope in such a state of love I was, though I would come to realize that I had been a madman."

At the beginning of the summer Henry won another victory over King Stephen. Stephen's son, Eustace, was appalled by his father's defeat. Eustace considered himself England's next heir, although nearly everyone considered him obnoxious and rude. Fortunately for England and Henry, Eustace died on August 17 after eating a dish of spoiled eels.

In faraway Aquitaine, on the same day as Eustace's death, Eleanor had a son she named William after the dukes of Aquitaine. Henry now had a male heir. The exciting news would take weeks to reach Henry in England. Riders on horseback could typically cover about twenty miles a day.

In this medieval drawing, a troubadour joins his lady love in a falconry expedition. Their horses seem coyly aware of the courtship at hand. *(Heidelberg University Library)*

After his son's death, King Stephen lost the will to fight. On November 6, 1153, he met with Henry and declared him the heir. All eyes turned to Henry to establish peace and improve England. Stephen took Henry to London, "where he was received with joy by enormous crowds and splendid processions. Thus, by God's mercy, peace dawned on the ruined realm of England, putting an end to its troubled night," said Henry of Huntingdon.

With the kingdom of England in his possession, Henry returned to Normandy. Eleanor joined him there with their eight-month-old son and met her formidable mother-in-law, Empress Matilda, for the first time. These two powerful women were wary of each other. Henry's reliance on his mother's advice exasperated Eleanor, who had her own strong opinions. Eleanor and Matilda had only a cool, formal relationship.

Although life with Henry was never easy, Eleanor was content. She was soon pregnant again, and even the feud with her ex-husband eased. Louis had married Constance, the daughter of the king of Castile in Spain. He had traveled to Spain by a circuitous route to avoid stepping foot in Eleanor's territory. Afterwards, he made overtures of friendship to Henry and the two reconciled. However, Eleanor still had no contact with her daughters, Marie and Alix.

In October of 1154, while Henry was away battling vassals in the Vexin, Eleanor received a message from England. After a nineteen-year reign, King Stephen died on October 25. His death ended a generation of misery and civil war in England. The message urged Henry to "come without delay and take possession of the kingdom." Henry returned home, and he and Eleanor quickly packed for their journey to England. Eleanor took forty-two richly embroidered gowns, fourteen pairs of shoes (many decorated with gold thread), and ten warm undershirts. They traveled with Eleanor's sister, Petronilla, whose husband Raoul had died in 1151. They were also accompanied by Henry's two brothers, nobles, and bishops. Matilda stayed behind to keep the peace.

After a frenzied two weeks of preparation, Eleanor and Henry rode nearly 150 miles to the windy harbor town of Barfleur in Normandy. The new addition to their kingdom waited across the English Channel.

5

Queen of England

The English Channel churned ominously with icy rain and high winds as Eleanor and Henry crossed to England in November 1154. It was a taste of what life would be like during her time in England.

England was a rural, feudal society. It had been invaded in 1066 by William the Conqueror of Normandy, who had defeated the Saxon king, Harold, at the Battle of Hastings. William and the Norman kings who followed him had strengthened the power of the crown and firmly established the feudal system in England.

In 1154, few of England's 2.5 million people lived in towns; most worked the land. The country was divided into shires controlled by shire reeves—sheriffs that represented the king, enforced justice, and collected taxes. The king and his advisers were the government, which meant the monarch's personality was vitally important. A strong, confident ruler would have the power and charisma to control his country, thwart rebellion, and keep advisers under his thumb. A weak ruler would be constantly threatened by hostile noblemen and power-hungry advisers.

Church feasts and holy days punctuated the year. The local church was the center of village social life. There were few governmental services. Monasteries cared for

This painting from the illuminated manuscript, *Le livre de la chasse* (The Book of Hunting), depicts a scene of everyday recreational activities during the Middle Ages. *(Bibliothèque Nationale, Paris)*

the poor and sick and sheltered travelers. They were also centers of learning, preserving ancient books and documents. Monks were trained in calligraphy and illumination, an art imported from the Byzantine Empire. They created Bibles and other books bound with leather-covered oak boards and decorated with gold. The printing press would not be invented for another three hundred years, so books were not available to the masses. They were painstakingly copied by hand. These labors of love were mainly religious in content and were rare and expensive. The majority of people could not read or write.

England had suffered from years of famine, the result of bad weather that destroyed crops and caused poor harvests. Despite eating roots, horses, and dogs in an attempt to survive, many people had still died.

When Henry arrived, England had been without a ruler for six weeks. The Archbishop of Canterbury, the leader of the Catholic Church in England, had been keeping the realm safe for Henry. Archbishop Theobald had supported Henry's mother's claim and helped to arrange the treaty declaring Henry to be King Stephen's heir. Under his watchful eye, no one dared dispute Henry's succession. Henry was eager to claim his throne. He and Eleanor had waited in Barfleur for a month for the stormy weather to ease before setting sail. But Henry's always-thin patience had cracked, and on December 6 he announced that they would sail at dawn, regardless of the weather.

The next day Eleanor, who was seven months pregnant, carried sixteen-month-old William onto the boat. The coast was dark with sleet and the winds whipped around her. Eleanor was carrying more than her children across the one-hundred-mile-wide English Channel. She also brought with her Aquitanian culture and ideals that she would spread to England. For a day and a night, the ships tossed in the sea, their feeble lantern lights lost in the murky dark. The ships landed, scattered along England's southern coast.

Upon Henry and Eleanor's arrival, the people in England were awed by Henry's defiance of the elements. Crowds of villagers lined the frozen roads, stamping their snowy, damp feet to keep warm. They hoped to catch a glimpse of their twenty-one-year-old king and the famous wife who had left a dull king to marry a bold, young warrior.

Eleven days later, Henry and Eleanor were crowned king and queen of England at Westminster Abbey in London. Henry became Henry II and was crowned with one of William the Conqueror's crowns; they both were anointed with holy oils. The solemn abbey sparkled with the gold and glittering stones that gleamed in everyone's clothes, from pages to knights to bishops. Eleanor and Henry dressed in elegant silk and gauze robes. As church bells rang in celebration, people cheered and ran alongside the royal procession crying, "Long live the king!" The reign of the Plantagenets had begun.

Eleanor and Henry lived outside of London while

Westminster Palace was renovated. The dinginess and dilapidation of the palace stood as a reminder of England's decay under Stephen. Eleanor had her second son soon after being crowned, on February 28, 1155. She named him Henry, after his father and great-grandfather.

From her windows, Eleanor could see the snowy curtain of winter envelope London. Wood smoke filled

Henry and Eleanor ride into the royal city of Westminster to claim the throne of England. *(Courtesy of the Granger Collection.)*

the air from the bonfires on the banks of the Thames River. Men and boys skated across frozen ponds using horses' shinbones as skates. The smells of fish, wool, and beer cut through the foggy, chilly air. Shops and wooden houses painted red, blue, and black lined the streets. On the outskirts of the city of 35,000, people hunted in the meadows and forests. One of London's most popular attractions was a public cook shop that served hot meals twenty-four hours a day.

Outside the city people supplemented their crops by fishing and hunting swans, peacock, venison, and hare. Vast acres of forest were set aside for the king and his family to hunt. Those caught poaching in the king's forest could be heavily fined. People ate fruits, berries, and herbs in season and wealthy families imported costly spices such as ginger, cloves, and cinnamon. Rich sauces and garlic helped cover the taste of less-than-fresh meats. Desserts were made of dried fruit, gingerbread, and spices. Only the wealthy used plates, usually sharing one between two people.

Henry's first goal as king was to establish an effective, uniform legal system. Under King Stephen, laws differed from town to town. Criminals suffered trial by ordeal. For example, a woman accused of a crime had to carry a hot iron for three steps. She was judged guilty if her burn was half the size of a walnut. Henry instituted trial by a jury of twelve men who knew the facts and swore the innocence or guilt of the accused. Henry and Eleanor also traveled throughout England so people could bring complaints to the royal court for trial. The king and queen's overseeing trials gave people confidence in the new legal system. The decisions of Henry's courts were used as precedents in similar cases in other courts. His reform of the English court system earned Henry the nickname "The Lion of Justice" and is one of the foundations of the development of British common law.

Henry also reorganized the monetary system. Although people were using money more and bartering less, only the silver penny was in circulation in England. Money was counted in shillings, marks, and pounds, but there were no actual coins in these amounts. Henry issued new coins in these denominations. Trade and

A coin from the time of Henry's reign. *(British Museum, London)*

wealth increased because of the uniform currency and stable justice system. Under Henry's steady, firm hand, order was soon established. Peace would reign in England for the next twenty years.

Henry had help reforming the political system. He had appointed a young, intelligent man named Thomas Becket as his chancellor, who had the task of writing letters and documents in the king's name. Becket was tall, dark-haired, and slender. Although he had a tendency to stutter, he could explain complicated subjects clearly. Becket was a capable, ambitious administrator with a strong sense of duty. Elegant, witty, and charming, he thrived in his public role as chancellor. Although Becket could be obstinate and manipulative, Henry instantly liked him and grew to depend on his intelligence and honesty.

Henry put Becket in charge of renovating Westminster Palace. Normally a job this large would have taken at least a year, but Becket hired an army of workers. The men finished the repairs within fifty days, although the noise they made was deafening. The old palace was converted to business offices and living quarters for courtiers. Gardens and thick woods surrounded the new palace. In the courtyard, as men polished hunting spears, Henry's shaggy wolfhounds frolicked. The new palace was large and functional, but it lacked elegance. Eleanor decorated the palace to her own tastes, making it more comfortable and regal. She bought tapestries and silk cushions and filled the rooms with oil lamps and incense. She imported exotic spices for the kitchen and wines, as she disliked heavy English beer.

Eleanor also noticed that her husband and Becket had become nearly inseparable. "The King and Becket played together like little boys of the same age, at the court, in church, in assemblies, in riding," said William Fitz-Stephen, a medieval writer who penned a biography of Thomas Becket.

To Eleanor's chagrin, Henry heaped riches and honors on Becket. She soon began to lose responsibilities, powers, and influence to Becket. As Henry had always disliked entertaining visitors, he shifted those duties to his chancellor as well. With his newfound wealth, Becket kept a splendid residence where he entertained, serving expensive foods on dainty dishes and drinks in silver goblets.

Eleanor also realized Henry was having affairs with other women. He even had an illegitimate son, Geoffrey, about the same age as William. Henry took him into their household to be raised with Eleanor's children, and she could not complain.

Henry was always hungry for more land. He considered conquering Ireland for his youngest brother William. Empress Matilda hurried to England from Normandy to convince him that Ireland was poor and not worth the fight. She also informed Henry that his brother Geoffrey was going to try to seize Anjou. Geoffrey complained that Henry should have ceded Anjou to him once he became king of England. But Henry had no intention of ceding any land to Geoffrey. He never willingly gave up land once he acquired it. So, instead of going to Ireland, Henry sailed for France to deal with his brother.

Eleanor was left behind with a stronger role. She supervised various governmental matters and traveled to check on royal lands. She journeyed through thick forests filled with wolves and wild boars and passed green hills dotted with sheep and cattle, fields of rye and wheat, thatched huts, and cities surrounded by thick walls. Traveling must have been uncomfortable, however; the queen was pregnant again.

In the spring of 1156, Eleanor's oldest son, three-year-old William, died. Whether he was sick for a long time or died of a sudden illness is unknown. It was not unusual for a young child to die. Children were especially vulnerable to scarlet fever, small pox, and dysentery. Although losing children to accidents and diseases was not rare, it was nevertheless painful. When Henry returned after stripping his brother of his castles and claims, he and Eleanor buried their small son at Reading Abbey. Henry's grandfather, Henry I, had founded the abbey, which rested between the Thames and Kennet Rivers west of London. The abbey held the sacred relic of St. James's hand, courtesy of Empress Matilda, who had pulled off the dead saint's hand while visiting his shrine in Spain. Pilgrims flocked to this relic, staying with the monks in the abbey's many buildings. Little William was buried at his great-grandfather's feet.

William had been the heir to England and Normandy. This role now passed to young Henry. In June, Eleanor had a daughter. She named her Matilda, in honor of Henry's mother.

Although Henry and Eleanor had worked hard in England, their greatest wealth and worst problems were in France. These widespread domains were becoming increasingly difficult to govern. Aquitaine, always in a simmering state of revolt, was a thorn in Henry's side and a source of friction between the king and queen. The rebels disliked Henry for his appointment of outsiders to key government positions. Henry had created central administrations in Westminster, England, and Rouen, Normandy, to consistently govern territories without common languages, laws, or customs. Eleanor did not agree with Henry's administrative policies. Although centralized government had worked for Normandy and England, she doubted it would in Aquitaine, given its tradition of independent nobles.

Henry would spend his entire life on the move, trying to keep his empire at peace. "Now in Ireland, now in England, now in Normandy, he must fly rather than travel by horse or ship!" commented King Louis. The French king still did not have an heir. His wife, Constance, had borne a daughter they named Marguerite; Louis now had three daughters and no sons. French law forbade succession by or through a woman. Louis was alarmed by the births of Eleanor's sons; she and Henry were creating a family dynasty to inherit their vast empire—and to threaten his.

Henry and Eleanor's nomadic court stayed in castles, palaces, abbeys, and hunting lodges. In London they frequented Westminster Palace, Windsor Castle, and the Tower of London. One of the family's favorite residences was their hunting lodge at Woodstock outside the city. They moved every few weeks. Sometimes they moved because of business or to go on hunting expeditions; sometimes it was so the castle could be cleaned. With 250 people using chamber pots, their residences quickly grew filthy and the smell unbearable. The court also consumed great quantities of food. After decimating the livestock and crops in an area, they moved on so the food could be replenished for their next visit.

In 1157, Henry set off on a great progress throughout England. Although Eleanor was pregnant again, she joined him. On September 8, 1157, she gave birth to her third son, Richard. Traditionally their oldest surviving son, Henry, would inherit the kingdom of England and the other territories, and his brothers would owe allegiance to him. Being a girl, Matilda would inherit little beyond the prospect of a political marriage to enhance her family's standing.

Eleanor, however, wanted Richard to be her heir as the duke of Aquitaine and the count of Poitou. Some remembered an ancient prophecy and thought it applied to Eleanor: "The Eagle of the Broken Covenant . . . will rejoice in her third nesting." The eagle, they reasoned, was Eleanor, and the broken covenant was her divorce from Louis. The third nesting was Richard, her third son.

Merlin and Arthur

It was said that the ancient wizard Merlin had made the prophecy predicting Richard's birth. According to legend, Merlin had been a famous sorcerer, adviser, and scholar with the ability to see into the future. One tale credited him with the magical construction of Stonehenge. Medieval writer Geoffrey of Monmouth was one of the first to write about Merlin. In his tales, the character of Merlin is a combination of two ancient British folktales: the story of a man named Myrddin who was called the "Wildman in the Woods" and the tale of a fatherless boy who predicted doom for a king. Stories also told of Merlin being accompanied by a wolf or bear, running with wild deer, and even flying. Supposedly born in 460 and dying in 580, Merlin's mother was a Welsh princess and his father was a demon.

Arthurian legend produced many works of art, including this image of Arthur drawing the sword, Excalibur, from a stone in the fourteenth-century text *The Romance of Merlin*. (British Library, London)

There are many inconsistencies in medieval tales. Sometimes Merlin is pictured as an elderly adviser to kings, other times he is evil. He was a popular figure of the Middle Ages, remembered both in spoken tales and in new written stories of adventure.

Eleanor and Henry were particularly fascinated with the tales of King Arthur, the legendary early king of Britain, who was mentored by Merlin. Legend said that Arthur had become king after pulling a sword named Excalibur from a stone. Many before him had tried and failed to free the sword. At Arthur's brilliant court in his castle Camelot, goodness and beauty reigned. Arthur gathered the greatest, most chivalrous knights in Europe around him, such as Sir Lancelot and Sir Galahad. Married to Queen Guenivere, in some ways Arthur was a tragic figure. His son Mordred became his great enemy and his wife had an affair with his favorite knight. According to legend, at the end of his life Arthur sailed to the mystical island of Avalon. Before he left he vowed to return someday, a promise that earned him the title the "Once and Future King."

Stories of Arthur and Merlin became popular in the twelfth century. Geoffrey of Monmouth first wrote about the legendary king around 1135 after collecting old Celtic legends. He was the first to associate Arthur with Merlin. Other authors in the Middle Ages followed his lead. Robert Wace wrote about Arthur's Round Table, where all knights were equal. Chrétien de Troyes, who was patronized by Eleanor's daughter Marie, wrote five poems based on Arthurian legends. He was the first to write about Camelot, the beautiful Guenivere, and the brave Sir Lancelot. Some people believe that Eleanor was the inspiration for the legends surrounding Guenivere.

The romantic Arthurian tales, set in enchanted castles, and full of brave conquests, provided an escape from the drudgery of daily feudal life. Because of Henry and Eleanor's interest in them, the tales spread throughout Christendom and it became fashionable to act like the characters. Henry instituted a search for Arthur's bones at Glastonbury in southern England. A lead cross and two skeletons believed to be those of Arthur and Guenivere were found in 1190. On the cross was written "Here lies Arthur, the famous king, in the Island of Avalon."

Whatever the reason, Richard was Eleanor's favorite from the beginning.

After Richard's birth Eleanor and Henry continued their tour, visiting every corner of their kingdom. In one year, they traveled over 3,500 miles. They passed over terrible roads, mere remnants of the ones left behind by the Romans centuries before. The roads turned to quagmire in wet weather. Eleanor traveled on horseback and in a brightly painted, barrel-shaped wagon with wooden wheels and a leather roof.

Despite the blistering pace, there was no schedule. Henry took everything he needed with him: parchment, documents, barrels of coins, boxes of jewels, and advisers. He often changed his mind or followed a whim, and chaos would ensue as servants struggled to fulfill his latest demand, busily loading wagons and pack animals with tables, plates, beds, cosmetics, and clothes. The court traveled with an army of courtiers, cooks, servants, jugglers, magicians, and court prostitutes. Messengers sped ahead to warn the king's tenants when the court was about to descend on them. As hosts, they were required to provide one night of entertainment for the entire court. Doing so financially ruined many. The physical discomforts of traveling did not bother Henry, but many complained about the dirt and misery. One courtier wrote:

> The king would turn aside to some other place which had perhaps one single dwelling with accommodation for himself and no one else. I hardly dare say it, but I

believe that in truth he took a delight in seeing what a fix he put us in. After wandering some three or four miles in an unknown wood, and often in the dark, we thought ourselves lucky if we stumbled upon some filthy hovel. There were often a sharp and bitter argument about a mere hut, and swords were drawn for possession of lodgings, which pigs would have shunned.

For Eleanor, the terrible food was the worst. The bread, meat, and fish were usually only half-cooked. Often the meat was rancid. There were some nights when the wine was so muddy the queen had to close her eyes and filter it through her clenched teeth. By the end of the year, Eleanor was pregnant again for the fifth time in six years. She thankfully ended the progress in London the following July.

During the progress, Henry had begun to scheme about marrying his son Henry to King Louis's daughter Marguerite. If Louis died without an heir, Henry thought he could take over the kingdom of France, despite French law forbidding succession to the throne by or through a female. In light of Louis's dislike and distrust of Eleanor and Henry, the betrothal scheme required both delicacy and nerve.

Henry sent Becket to Paris as his ambassador. Intending to awe the French, Becket arrived with rich gifts, chests of gold, barrels of ale, and twenty-four changes of clothes. Each wagon was surrounded by huge dogs, and the horses all carried monkeys on their backs. "Marvellous is the King of the English whose chancellor goes thus and so grandly," one awed Parisian commented.

Becket was received like a prince, and Louis surprisingly agreed to the betrothal. Henry and Louis met in the Vexin to finalize the terms. Louis handed over his six-month-old daughter to Henry after demanding that Eleanor have no hand in her upbringing. Louis also gave his daughter the Vexin and its castles. As a sign of their agreement, Henry and Louis traveled to Normandy to the abbey of Mont-Saint-Michel. With the ocean tide lapping in the background, the two kings said mass and dined together. Louis returned to Paris convinced their rift was over—but peace between them would not last long.

On September 23, 1158, Eleanor gave birth to another son. She named him Geoffrey. The queen immediately went back to work, governing England while Henry was away. Nurses fed her children, comforting them when they cried and teaching them to speak. The women even chewed the royal children's meat before they grew teeth.

Eleanor's role was to provide heirs and to be present at banquets and ceremonies. Henry did allow her some independence in making decisions and responsibility in administrative matters when he was absent. Eleanor also implemented Henry's orders and settled disputes. She sometimes presided over the courts and dispensed justice, and she was constantly on the move, traveling throughout England and Normandy, unfazed by stormy seas or roads lurking with danger. Eleanor zealously upheld Henry's policies and ruled with an imperious, confident hand, but like other women in the Middle Ages, she was aware that her husband held ultimate control.

Although Eleanor was wealthy in her own right, Henry tightly monitored her finances. He had given her several manors to use but any income they produced went to the royal treasury, not to her personally. She had two sources of income. She was the first English queen granted the right to claim queen gold, an additional fee collected on certain payments made to the king. For every one hundred marks a person paid to the king, they were also required to pay Eleanor one gold mark. She hired her own officers to collect this unpopular fee. The sheriffs, in whose territories she resided, also were required to pay her dues.

In addition to being singers and instrumentalists, the troubadours of Eleanor's era were also skilled as poets. Typical subjects of troubador songs were war, chivalry, and courtly love. *(Bibliothèque Nationale, Paris)*

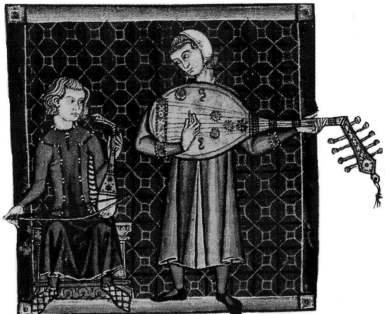

Eleanor continued to support art, poetry, and music. Her patronage of troubadours and other literary figures helped disperse the sophisticated southern French cultural traditions throughout the Angevin empire. Writers and poets dedicated their works to Eleanor. Although she had difficulty imposing more civilized manners on Henry's court, she did lay down some ground rules of courtesy. No man could appear before her with uncombed hair, for example. When she was not fulfilling administrative duties, she read books and poetry, listened to music, prayed, and attended to family and household matters.

Henry and Eleanor had considerable influence over their court and all of Europe. Henry was said to have more education than any other ruler of his time. He enjoyed talking with the best scholars, discussing intellectual problems, and reading for pleasure. The king and queen's interests added to the burgeoning twelfth-century Renaissance that was shaping Europe. As their children grew, traveled, and married, they too would help spread this literary culture.

In September of 1160, Eleanor took two of her children, Henry and Matilda, to Normandy. King Louis's wife was about to have another child. If the baby was a boy, Henry wanted Matilda betrothed to him. However, before dying in childbirth, Queen Constance had a daughter she named Alys. Desperate for a male heir, Louis quickly married Adela of Champagne, the sister of Count Theobald of Blois and Count Henry of

Champagne, both men hostile to Henry. They were related to King Stephen, who had usurped the throne from Henry's mother.

Worried they would convince Louis to stop the marriage of Louis's daughter to his heir, Henry decided to marry the children immediately. Five-year-old Henry was married to three-year-old Marguerite. Louis was furious. Henry then claimed Marguerite's dowry of the Vexin territory and began fortifying its castles against attack. Louis and Count Theobald retaliated by attempting to threaten Henry's territory of Tourraine, southwest of the kingdom of France. This effort failed when Henry, who had been anticipating this move, marched in and seized the castle. Louis quickly realized opposing Henry was futile and ended the dispute before winter.

When the conflict ended, Eleanor and Henry began rebuilding churches, monasteries, and castles. Eleanor donated money to several religious institutions in Poitou and Aquitaine, such as the Gothic church of Notre-Dame-la-Grande, in which she and Henry commissioned stained-glass windows of themselves. Eleanor also had the city walls and bridges of Poitiers rebuilt. She added a spacious hall to her family's castle, along with large arched windows that revealed the distant green hills and valley and the blue river encircling the town. The abbey of Fontevraud benefited the most. Eleanor funded the abbey's new octagonal kitchen with five fireplaces and twenty chimneys. The kitchen provided food for its community and guests, often serving nearly one thousand people. Eleanor would continue to give generous gifts to the abbey. Thanks to her, Fontevraud's prestige increased from a house of refuge to an aristocratic institution, fashionable with the daughters of knights and nobles.

Eleanor was soon pregnant again. In September of 1161, she gave birth to her second daughter with Henry, naming the baby Eleanor. The queen then turned her attention to her oldest son. He was six years old and a married man. Many were shocked he still lived with his parents and had not begun his education. Young Henry was sent to live with Becket, who would serve as his tutor. Eleanor sadly watched her son, like her husband, fall under Becket's spell. As much as she loved and admired her husband, Henry's mistakes with his family were becoming apparent. Henry was delighted with each new baby and he spoiled them with gifts of money, lands, and titles. They had little responsibility. Henry's children were pawns for him to increase his own power through marriage contracts. He failed to prepare them for the future.

Henry was eyeing another position for Becket. Archbishop Theobald of Canterbury had recently died. The Archbishop of Canterbury outranked all other clergymen in England and had absolute power over the Church in England. Only the pope was his superior in the Church. Henry had plans to radically curb the Church's power. One of Henry's goals was to reform the ecclesiastical courts, which he thought did little to punish clerics who committed crimes. Most people were tried in the king's courts, but clergymen were tried by the Church. Henry's courts doled out severe punishments, while church courts delivered light penalties. As Archbishop of Canterbury, Becket could further Henry's schemes.

The appointment of high church officials such as archbishops by secular rulers was called lay investiture. The practice had led to conflicts between popes and

King Henry II argues with Thomas Becket in this illustrated page of Latin text from *Chronicle of England* by Peter of Langtoft. Henry touches his left hand with his right forefinger as if admonishing the archbishop, who stands holding a staff with a cross and gestures back. *(Courtesy of Art Resource.)*

rulers in the past. It was established practice in England. However, once a man was raised to such a high position in the Church, he was often in conflict with the men who had appointed him. The interests of the church and the state often conflicted, and the archbishop was duty-bound to side with the Church.

The king summoned Becket to Normandy. When he arrived, Henry revealed his idea. Becket was not pleased. He knew Henry's plans for the Church. If he appointed Becket archbishop, Henry would put his friend in the terrible position of either acting as the king's puppet or fulfilling his duty to the Church and opposing Henry's reforms. Becket begged Henry to reconsider, knowing he would eventually either displease God or the king. "The love which is now so great between us would be changed into the most bitter hatred. I know that you would make demands that I could never meet," Becket said.

Stubborn Henry ignored Becket's protests. It was a fateful decision that turned his most trusted friend and aide into his greatest enemy—and led to one of the most famous murders in European history.

6

Betrayal and Murder

By the time Eleanor and Henry returned to England in January 1163, she had been gone two years. She was almost forty years old and her relationship with Henry was changing. As his ambitions focused on arranging marriages for his children and on laying claim to the French throne, she was pushed to the background. Increasingly, she was merely Henry's aging wife. Eleanor was not happy with the change.

Henry's stubbornness and all-consuming ambition had created a bigger problem for him than an unhappy wife. Becoming Archbishop of Canterbury had changed Thomas Becket from a worldly courtier into a strict man of the cloth whose focus and allegiance was to the Catholic Church, not Henry's ambitions.

Henry wanted to bring the English Church under

royal control. The conflict centered on the role of the church courts. He wanted to retry church officials after the church court had dealt with them. A murderer, for example, tried in a church court might only be defrocked. Henry thought they should face a more severe punishment. Becket refused to go along with Henry's plans. He claimed that doing so would expose the clergy to double jeopardy.

The larger issue was the conflict between the emergence of a powerful, efficient secular government and the international Catholic Church. This conflict between secular rulers and the Church had been taking place in other parts of Europe for some time and would continue into the modern era.

Becket had replaced his expensive clothes with a monk's habit and, according to Herbert of Bosham, wore "a hair shirt of the roughest kind, which reached to his knees and swarmed with vermin." Henry had put Becket in the position of having to choose between his king and his God, and Becket had made his choice. Now wholly dedicated to the Church, one of Becket's first actions had been to resign as Henry's chancellor. He was determined to protect the Church from any attempt by Henry to erode its power.

Henry claimed the supremacy of the royal courts was actually a reversion to a precedent established by his grandfather, Henry I. But it was not a tradition anyone remembered, and there is little evidence that Henry I had actually attempted to carry out this policy. Becket knew there were abuses in church courts, but as archbishop he did not want to do anything to limit the Church's power. He and his bishops opposed Henry, and each side dug in its heels. "By the eyes of God!" thundered Henry, "I demand absolute and express agreement to my customs."

When Becket refused, Henry confiscated Becket's manors and removed his son from the archbishop's care. This was the beginning of six years of bitter disputes.

As Henry and Eleanor spitefully celebrated Christmas in one of Becket's former homes, the archbishop defied Henry by seeing that even serious crimes received light punishments in church courts. Henry appealed to Pope Alexander III, who owed him gratitude

Pope Alexander III, elected in 1159, was caught between Henry II and Thomas Becket during their disagreement over the rights and privileges of the Church. *(Palazzo Pubblico, Siena)*

for supporting him against an antipope who was dividing the Church. The pope also did not believe Henry was proposing anything that went against the teachings of the Church. Pope Alexander thought that Becket had insulted the prideful king, who could not afford to lose face. As Becket's support faded, the pope urged him to submit to Henry; the archbishop acknowledged defeat. But the enraged Henry wanted Becket's submission made public.

In January of 1164, Henry summoned the archbishops and nobles of the realm to his hunting lodge of Clarendon near Salisbury in southern England. There Henry produced a document, the Constitution of Clarendon, which he said listed the laws of the land that were observed during his grandfather's reign. Actually, many of the listed laws were Henry's own reforms. The constitution would effectively place the Catholic Church in England under the crown's control. For example, clergymen were forbidden to leave the realm without the king's permission and could not appeal his decisions to the pope. Becket refused to sign. He stalked out of the hall, clutching a copy of the constitution, and growling that he would never concede to its demands.

Henry had elevated his quarrel with Becket beyond the point of compromise. Although reluctant to offend the powerful Henry, Pope Alexander III condemned the Constitution of Clarendon.

Henry set out to ruin Becket. He demanded that Becket return all the money he had received as chancellor.

Seeing that it was an amount far beyond what he could pay, Becket fled to Flanders. "We have not finished with him yet!" Henry said when he learned of Becket's escape.

That winter Henry banished Becket's relatives from England. Stripped of their possessions, four hundred people of all ages were packed onto boats headed for Flanders, where they began life again as beggars. The cruel act did not surprise Eleanor, but it did cause her to despair. Again Henry was allowing his personal feelings to control his actions. He was obsessed with vengeance and was close to becoming the sort of tyrant Eleanor could not admire.

Becket portrayed himself to the pope as the victim of Henry's attacks on the Church. He wrote to European rulers and asked for their support. Before long, much of Europe believed Henry was persecuting Becket and the Church. The pope felt secure enough to threaten Henry with excommunication.

Henry only grew more enraged. "The king, burning with his customary fury, threw the cap from his head, undid his belt, threw far from him the cloak and robes in which he was dressed, with his own hands tore the silken coverlet off the bed, and, sitting down as though on a dung heap, began to chew the straw of the mattress," wrote John of Salisbury.

Henry worked to put pressure on the pope to abandon Becket. He formed an alliance with German emperor Frederick Barbarossa and betrothed his daughter

Matilda to the emperor's cousin. He also betrothed three-year-old Eleanor to the emperor's infant son. This was a powerful alliance that threatened the other kings in Europe. Emperor Frederick Barbarossa had championed Pope Alexander's rival in the earlier struggle. Frederick disliked Alexander so strongly that when the antipope died he perpetuated the division in the Church by supporting another rival. Clearly, Alexander had lost Henry's support. The alliance also succeeded in surrounding his old enemy, King Louis of France, who had been sympathetic to Becket. Although no doubt influenced by his strong devotion to the Church, Louis had also seized the opportunity to weaken Henry's prestige in Europe by offering Becket asylum and support.

Henry was consumed with anger at Becket, like a child throwing a temper tantrum. Despite her dislike of Becket, Eleanor stayed out of the argument. She might have been distracted because she was pregnant again.

Henry's fight with Becket in England affected the rest of his holdings. Becket's intransigence revealed that Henry could be defied. Noblemen in Normandy, Anjou, Poitou, and Aquitaine, tired of Henry's domineering, were poised for rebellion. Henry decided to set out on a mission to teach a lesson to those who opposed him.

In May of 1165, Eleanor traveled to Anjou, where Henry left her in charge of the territories of Anjou and Maine while he charged off after the rebels over the next few months.

King Louis was openly conspiring with Henry's

Dressed in a full suit of chain mail, perhaps in preparation for a crusade, a young knight kneels in service to his overlord. *(British Library, London)*

enemies. In August of 1165, Louis's third wife had finally bore him an heir, he named the boy Philip. The French nicknamed the prince Dieu-Donné, "God-given." Louis was more determined than ever to stand up to Henry's encroachments into France. He intended to preserve his kingdom for his son.

In an attempt both to display his strength and to

soothe his vassals in Aquitaine, Henry summoned a council. He presented them with their future overlord, young Henry, who would inherit England, Anjou, Normandy, and Aquitaine. Eleanor did not accompany Henry to her homeland; she opposed his decision. She still wanted her favorite son, Richard, to be granted Aquitaine. The people of Aquitaine were unimpressed with Henry's gesture and continued plotting against him. Henry was angry at Eleanor, considering her dissent a betrayal. She returned to England, and the rift between them grew.

Henry was not present when Eleanor's last daughter, Joanna, was born in October of 1165. He did not return at Christmas, either, and offered no explanation for his absence. He returned in the spring and Eleanor was soon pregnant again; this would be the last time.

Eleanor stayed busy preparing for her daughter Matilda's marriage. She ensured that her daughter traveled in style, with twenty saddlebags filled with costly clothes and furs, and accompanied her to the ship that would take her to Germany. Matilda was eleven when she married her thirty-six-year-old fiancé. The age difference was enormous, even for the twelfth century. But her marriage helped expand trade between the two empires. Eleanor and Louis's daughters, Marie and Alix, had both married two years earlier in 1164.

Shortly before Christmas in 1166, Eleanor traveled to Woodstock, where she suffered a nasty shock. Living in the lodge like a queen was Henry's mistress, Rosamund de Clifford. Although Henry had many affairs, no mistress had ever occupied Eleanor's rooms before. An angry Eleanor hurried back to Oxford.

On Christmas Eve, Eleanor gave birth to a son named John. She spent Christmas with her infant and young children. She and Henry had been growing apart for many years, and it was sometime during this winter that she decided to separate from Henry and to return to her beloved home in Poitiers. She would not watch another woman assume her role as queen.

Henry's relationship with Rosamund was different from the affairs he had with earlier mistresses. His relationship with Rosamund lasted until she died ten years later. The "Fair Rosamund" inspired many legends, both about her affair with the king and her death. One of the most famous tales is about Henry's jealousy. According to legend, Henry hid Rosamund in the middle of a thick forest, in a strong, stone tower with 150 doors and a maze. Another legend was that Eleanor took revenge on Rosamund while Henry was away. According to the story, Eleanor found her way through the maze by following a silk string that had fallen from a sewing chest Henry had given his mistress. Eleanor offered Rosamund her choice of death, either by drinking a bowl of poison or by a dagger. Rosamund, as brave as she was beautiful, chose the poison. Another more gruesome tale told of Eleanor bleeding Henry's mistress to death by placing two toads on Rosamund's chest. As the toads sucked at Rosamund, draining her blood, Eleanor

Paintings such as this one, created in 1862 by Edward Burne-Jones, have perpetuated the stories of the clash between Fair Rosamund *(right)* and Queen Eleanor *(left)*. *(Courtesy of Art Resource.)*

cackled. There is no evidence to support any of these stories, and little is known about Henry's "Fair Rosamund".

Eleanor had been with Henry fourteen years and bore him seven children. Henry had always expected Eleanor to submit to his will and rarely sought her advice or allowed her to interfere in politics. For a woman like Eleanor this had been difficult.

At Christmas, Eleanor informed Henry she was leaving. She tactfully suggested her presence in Poitiers could help calm the nobles in Aquitaine, where rebellion still smoldered. Henry had been unable to stamp out the rebellions there; some vassals had even offered their allegiance to Louis. Henry agreed to Eleanor's plan, and the couple unofficially separated.

Eleanor packed her belongings and returned home to Aquitaine. Her new household in Poitiers swarmed with young people—knights, ladies-in-waiting, her own handsome sons and beautiful daughters, and her future daughters-in-law, Constance of Brittany and Alys. Young Eleanor would soon marry the king of Castile, and Joanna was engaged to the future king of Sicily. However, her son John, nicknamed Lackland for his lack of inheritance, lived at the abbey in nearby Fontevraud. Eleanor and Henry had sent him to live there to dedicate several years of his life to the Church.

For years Eleanor's children had been dragged from one castle to the next without one or both parents. Now Eleanor drew them together to the halls and gardens of her childhood. They were surrounded by troubadours and entertainers. Eleanor's court became an oasis of freedom for women of independence and imagination.

Forty-six years old in 1167, Eleanor was old by medieval standards. But she was not ready to retire. She still traveled frequently, but returning to her well-lit, elegant castle was always a joy. Unlike the damp, smoky castles of England, sunlight poured in through the arched windows of Eleanor's home. She decided to cut Aquitaine off from Henry's empire. She wanted to control its future, to turn Aquitaine and Poitiers into splendid cultural centers, and, most importantly, to place her son Richard on the throne.

Eleanor began to try to heal the wounds caused by thirty years of rule by foreign overlords. She traveled through Aquitaine and dismissed Henry's unpopular administrators. She encouraged exiled nobles to return home, restored their lands to them, and revived old fairs and customs.

Constant rumors about the king and queen's relationship circulated throughout the land, but Eleanor was enjoying her independence. She preferred living in her native lands as a duchess with freedom rather than as Henry's subordinate. Her living apart from Henry seemed to suit everyone's interests and calmed turbulent Aquitaine. Richard traveled at her side, gradually learning how she ruled. Henry, too, seemed content. He had rid himself of a wife he no longer wanted. As long as Eleanor cooperated with his plans, he was satisfied.

On January 6, 1169, Henry and Louis met once again to try to secure peace between their two kingdoms. Louis urged Henry to split his lands between his sons, knowing that Henry's empire would be weaker if it were divided. In the Treaty of Montmirail, they carved up Henry's realm. This frequent switching of inheritances was part of noble life in the Middle Ages, due to ongoing power struggles over land and the fact that heirs often died young. Henry also used his lands to control his children, vassals, and relationships with other kingdoms and territories. He wanted to provide for his sons after his death without them fighting for their inheritances. Furthermore, he realized his far-flung collection of territories was becoming difficult to manage.

Henry had little confidence that his sons could rule as he did. If he divided the empire it would be easier to administrate. He decided that young Henry would inherit England, Normandy, and Anjou. Geoffrey would inherit Brittany and be young Henry's vassal. Richard would receive Aquitaine and be Louis's vassal. Louis also agreed to betroth his daughter Alys to Richard. Louis turned his young daughter over to Henry, who became her guardian. Eleanor worried Louis was dividing and conquering Henry's empire by diplomacy. But Henry would not be deterred.

The agreement between Henry and Louis did not last long. Louis soon allied himself with one of Henry's enemies, William the Lion, the king of Scotland. It was the first in a long tradition of French-Scottish friendships threatening England.

The year 1170 began well for Eleanor and her family. Thirteen-year-old Richard had become the duke of a peaceful Aquitaine. Henry made plans for fifteen-year-old young Henry to be crowned as king of England, adopting the French custom of crowning the heir during his father's lifetime. It was the Archbishop of Canterbury's exclusive privilege to coronate the kings of England, but Becket and Henry were still feuding. Henry made plans for another archbishop to carry out the coronation. This was an insult to Becket and offended many others. Traditionally, crowning kings was the archbishop's religious duty; it symbolized the supremacy of the Church over any secular government. Furthermore, Louis was insulted because his daughter, Marguerite, young Henry's wife, was not included in the ceremony.

Becket refused to back down and, with the pope's blessing, warned that any bishops who participated in the coronation would be excommunicated. Henry stubbornly insisted on coercing bishops into defying the pope. Young Henry was crowned at Westminster Abbey on June 14.

The coronation of young Henry caused an uproar, fueling the tensions over Henry's domain. Ever stubborn, Henry was beginning to realize how disastrous the feud with Becket had become. His subjects, and now most of the Church, opposed him. He was in a dangerous situation. When the pope insisted that Henry and Becket end their dispute, Henry seized the chance to make peace. He admitted he had been wrong and asked Becket to return to Canterbury and re-crown young Henry and his wife Marguerite. "Come, my archbishop," Henry wrote to Becket. "Let us renew our ancient love for one another; let us show each other all the good we can and forget our old quarrel."

Becket agreed to Henry's plan, but he was still furious at the bishops who had crowned young Henry. He also did not trust Henry and thought the king meant to harm him. Before Becket returned to Canterbury he sent

Henry II and Eleanor's son, Henry the Young King. *(Rouen Cathedral)*

letters from the pope excommunicating the bishops who had performed the coronation. The excommunicated bishops complained to Henry, who was spending Christmas near Bayeux in northern Normandy. The bishops lied to enhance their pleas and told him Becket was leading an army through England.

The report from the bishops enraged Henry. "My lord, while Thomas lives, you will not have peace or quiet, or see good days," one of the men said. Exasperated, Henry's angry, wild words carried over the din of his guests. "Will no one rid me of this turbulent priest?" he supposedly cried.

This nineteenth-century French engraving imagines the murder of Thomas Becket at Canterbury Cathedral on December 29, 1170, by knights from the court of King Henry II. *(Courtesy of the Granger Collection.)*

Apparently, no one noticed when four of Henry's knights slipped from the noisy hall and headed for Canterbury in southeastern England. When Henry discovered they were missing, he realized they intended to rid him of Becket. He sent messengers to call them back, but they were already across the English Channel.

On December 29, the four knights appeared at Canterbury Cathedral and threatened to punish Becket if he did not flee England. When Becket told them to leave and to stop insulting the archbishop, the knights went into the courtyard muttering insults. That evening, when the monks went into the cathedral, the knights followed them inside.

"Where is Thomas Becket, traitor to the king and realm?" they cried.

Becket replied he was a priest and not a traitor to the king. The knights attacked him with their swords until one called out, "Let us away, knights; he will rise no more."

Like shadows, the four assassins fled into the night as Becket's blood slowly spread over the marble floor. Thomas Becket was dead, and Eleanor and Henry's world would never be the same again.

7

Rebellion

Word of Becket's murder spread like wildfire across Europe in the early days of 1171. Henry, horrified when he heard the news, spent six weeks grieving in seclusion. Eleanor could not comfort him; she was as shocked as everyone else. It was called the worst atrocity since Jesus Christ was crucified. Becket was the spiritual voice of England and the representative of the Catholic Church. To have such a man murdered would surely condemn Henry to Hell.

Becket became more powerful dead than he had been alive. Public opinion was that he had been slain in his church for doing his duty. Becket was now a martyr to the king's worldly ambition. Pilgrims hurried to Canterbury to smear themselves with his blood or to take it away in vials. They snipped off pieces of his clothes.

By Easter, there were claims of miracles witnessed at his tomb.

Henry was reviled. The passing years did little to improve his reputation. Even if not guilty of ordering the killing, his violent frustration had prompted the murder of a man who had once been his best friend. The pope forbade Henry to go on church property and excommunicated the knights. Henry did not punish the killers,

The pilgrimage to Canterbury to pay homage to Thomas Becket became a popular trek in Christendom almost immediately following Becket's death. Geoffrey Chaucer further popularized the progress in his fourteenth-century book *The Canterbury Tales,* which is told from the perspective of a group of pilgrims on the way to visit Becket's shrine. *(Library of Congress)*

which further convinced many they had acted on his orders.

The murder changed Eleanor's relationship with Henry. Their separation had been friendly and Eleanor had supported her husband throughout his quarrel with Becket, but brutally murdering the archbishop was another matter. The long-seething anger and frustration she had felt toward Henry turned to revulsion.

Fearing excommunication, Henry retreated to Ireland until tempers cooled. There he took over large tracts of land and reformed the Irish Church in an attempt to regain the pope's favor.

When Henry returned from Ireland he admitted to the pope that his angry words had prompted the four knights to murder Becket. Dressed in a hair shirt, Henry knelt and was whipped by monks to absolve him of his guilt. But he could not escape Becket, whose image was everywhere. On February 21, 1172, the pope made Becket a saint. His shrine in Canterbury became the most popular place of pilgrimage in Europe.

Eleanor now shared a contempt for Henry with her former husband Louis. Eleanor's three oldest boys were also deeply affected by Becket's murder. They began to turn against their father. Although they had respected their father before, they had never been close and had feared his terrifying rages. The three boys were no longer children. At seventeen, fifteen, and fourteen years old, they were anxious to be their own men and to take their place in society.

However, Henry still saw them as children. He honored them with titles but clung to his authority and money. Eleanor recognized her sons were immature but she understood their impatience. There would be no peace until Henry gave them power and responsibility.

Young Henry was handsome, popular, and charming. Generous and extravagant, he was also untrustworthy. Richard was tall and graceful with auburn hair and piercing blue eyes. He loved music and was ambitious and daring. Geoffrey, short and dark, was the most intelligent, but was also dangerous and treacherous. All three boys were well educated and had savage tempers they often unleashed against each other.

The boys were upset when Henry changed his mind about dedicating five-year-old John to the Catholic Church. Henry wanted to further expand his empire, and he saw a way to use John to acquire more land. When Count Humbert of Maurienne (a territory between Italy and Germany) suggested they form an alliance, he offered to marry his daughter Alice to John, the only one of Henry's sons not already betrothed. John would inherit Humbert's lands, giving the Anjous control of strategic western Alpine passes. None of John's older brothers begrudged him the marriage, but when Henry also gave John some lands and castles promised to young Henry, the prince was furious. His father-in-law, Louis, eager to foster conflict, advised him to demand his share. King Henry knew Louis was plotting against him and demanded that his son join him for Christmas.

Young Henry refused. He celebrated the holiday by throwing an extravagant feast for 110 of his knights in England.

Eleanor supported young Henry's cause. Henry's heavy-handed authority and loss of prestige from Becket's murder had caused large numbers of vassals to desert him, especially in southern France. Rebellion was brewing and she had no intention of being on her husband's side.

Eleanor wanted justice for her sons and more power for herself, even if her husband had to be removed from the political scene. Her sons hungered to rule their own lands, even if it meant overthrowing their father. The vassals desired an end to Henry's dictatorial government and would support anyone else. Louis fervently hoped to undermine the Anjou power that had been threatening him for years, even if he had to ally with his former wife.

Eleanor still had duties to perform as Henry's wife. Late in February of 1173, they hosted a week of banquets and festivities together in honor of John's betrothal to four-year-old Alice. Young Henry was present and took the opportunity to make public his unhappiness about his father's refusal to delegate power to him and his brothers. In a loud speech, he complained about the lands his father gave John and insisted his father had no right to take them without his consent. When Henry again refused his demands, young Henry ominously said Louis and the other nobles in England and Normandy agreed with him. Henry guessed forces were conspiring against him but did not realize Eleanor was in league with them. One of the guests, Eleanor's old enemy Count Raymond of Toulouse, took Henry aside. "I advise you, King, to beware of your wife and sons," he said.

Henry refused to believe Eleanor would plan a rebellion against him. Such a betrayal by a wife was unthinkable. Instead, Henry took action against the young king, vowing not to let young Henry out of his sight. Henry took his oldest son to Normandy and insisted they sleep in the same room. On March 5, while his father slept, young Henry persuaded the guards to lower the drawbridge, and he escaped. When Henry awoke and found his son missing, he chased after him but could not catch him. The escape had been well planned, with fresh horses waiting along the route to Paris.

Henry's worst fears were confirmed when his son and Louis joined forces. Young Henry had secretly visited Richard and Geoffrey, who were living with Eleanor. Soon after, the three brothers traveled together to Paris and joined in the rebellion. Eleanor encouraged southern lords to support Henry's overthrow.

Young Henry and his brothers promised land and money to anyone who would ally with them. The rebel coalition swelled to include King Louis, several French nobles, and the king of Scotland. Henry was left with six-year-old John, his illegitimate son Geoffrey, and the support of most of his vassals in Normandy and England.

Henry continued to hear rumors of Eleanor's disloyalty. He sent spies to infiltrate her court and commanded one of his archbishops to remind Eleanor of her duty as a wife. Hoping to return Eleanor to her senses, the archbishop wrote, "Return, O illustrious queen, to your husband, whom you must obey and with whom it is your duty to live."

Eleanor had no intention of returning to Henry or of abandoning her sons' cause. By late spring she decided she would be safer in Paris. Disguising herself in men's clothes, Eleanor attempted to escape, but she was discovered north of Poitou by some of the few men still loyal to Henry. She was captured and taken to the king, who whisked her away. For months Eleanor's whereabouts were unknown to her sons and her supporters. Ominously, Henry disbanded her court and nothing more was heard from her.

For Henry, Eleanor's betrayal was bitter, and he exacted a thorough vengeance. She was imprisoned and frequently moved between fortresses so no one knew her location. Eleanor had gambled and lost, but her sons were still free.

Throughout the summer, Henry fought against his sons. Young Henry was inexperienced at battle. Louis stepped in to take charge, but he was no match for King Henry, who gradually regained control. With speed and skill, he beat back the rebel groups one at a time, but his lands continued to seethe with revolt.

Henry began to see his setbacks as a punishment from

God for Becket's murder. In June of 1174, he sailed for England with Eleanor, who had not been seen in the year since her capture. After a meal of bread and water, she was imprisoned at Sarum Castle near Salisbury. Her life

Sarum Castle, where Eleanor was held for more than a decade. *(Bibliothèque Nationale, Paris)*

there was bleak. Water was scarce, and howling winds crossed the plains and swirled around the castle.

Henry rode to Canterbury and prostrated himself before Becket's tomb, praying for forgiveness. Then he was whipped by seventy monks and received a vial of Becket's blood. Sore and exhausted, Henry had just fallen asleep when he received news that his army had captured the king of Scotland. Henry had not expected God's forgiveness so soon. He and everyone else believed his victory came from Becket's forgiveness and intervention from the beyond.

Henry's enemies began to lose confidence. His sons and King Louis conceded defeat. In the peace treaty of Montlouis, Henry gave allowances and two castles to each of his sons but did not relinquish any power. Young Henry, Richard, and Henry's legitimate son Geoffrey promised to make no more demands. Henry excused their treason because they were young and had been led astray by Eleanor and Louis. But Henry and his sons would never completely trust each other again.

Henry released all of his hostages except Eleanor. She remained imprisoned as punishment for her influence over their sons. For the rest of Henry's life she would remain under guard in the strongly fortified towns of Winchester and Sarum. She had little contact with her children and was cut off from the outside world. Back in Poitou and Aquitaine her imprisonment provoked grief and anger.

With Eleanor jailed, Henry began to live openly with

Rosamund. "The King, who had long been a secret adulterer, now blatantly flaunted his paramour for all to see," wrote Gerald of Wales. "And since the world copies a king, he offended not only by his behavior but even more by his bad example."

When Rosamund died, Henry had a beautiful tomb built in a convent. When a bishop saw Rosamund's tomb, he ordered that she be reburied outside of the church because he said she was a harlot.

Henry began to take steps to have his marriage to Eleanor annulled, a move with far-reaching political consequences. If the pope annulled their marriage, Eleanor's lands would revert to her and her sons. She also would no longer be Henry's subject, which meant he could not keep her imprisoned. Returned to Aquitaine, she might scheme or marry a man who was Henry's enemy. Henry asked the pope to send a representative to hear his case. He and Eleanor, like Louis and Eleanor, were related. They shared a distant relative from early in the eleventh century. Henry loaded the pope's representative with silver in an attempt to bribe him. The king's plan was for Eleanor to consent to an annulment and become a nun at Fontevraud. That way, Henry would not have to return her lands. But Eleanor did not want to become a nun or to give up her inheritance. She appealed to the Archbishop of Rouen, who refused to have Eleanor committed to Fontevraud against her will.

Confident of an eventual annulment from the pope, Henry began to carry on an affair that had disastrous consequences for both the French and English thrones. Louis's daughter, Alys, who had been living at the court since she was a little girl, caught Henry's eye. Although the royal princess was supposed to marry his son Richard, Henry pursued the scandalous affair. It was rumored he intended to divorce Eleanor and make Alys queen of England. Henry might disinherit Eleanor's sons and raise new sons with Alys, or name John his sole heir. Henry thought John was too young to have been poisoned against him by Eleanor.

At sixteen years old, John made a charming first impression. He had red, curly hair, was well educated, and loved to read. But John was also greedy and ruthless and seemed to take pleasure in destroying lives. Later in his life he would set fire to six Scottish border towns and order his men to torture the inhabitants. Like his promiscuous father, he kept a series of mistresses and was rumored to resort to rape when his advances were rejected. "Foul as it is, Hell itself is defiled in the very presence of John," wrote thirteenth-century chronicler Matthew Paris.

By now, rumors of Henry and Alys's affair were circulating throughout Europe. Louis had either heard about the affair or been told of it by his daughter. Not wanting his princess daughter to be a king's common mistress, Louis demanded that Richard and Alys marry immediately and appealed to the pope to enforce the marriage. The pope, who had formerly rejected Henry's request for an annulment from Eleanor, now agreed—

but Henry resisted. Over the next few years, Henry quietly continued his affair with Alys while still promising that the marriage between Richard and Alys would soon take place. Alys secretly had a son and a daughter with Henry. Richard kept quiet; he had no intention of marrying Alys.

In 1179 Louis suffered a major stroke, and his fourteen-year-old son, Philip, was crowned king of France. Louis died on September 18, 1180. Philip burned with an ambition to incorporate Henry's empire into the French crown. He soon became a clever, calculating ruler.

Eleanor's sons began to quarrel again. Richard had been forced to put down several revolts by Aquitainian nobles angered at Eleanor's imprisonment. His brutal rule had earned his vassals' hatred. They plotted to overthrow him and offered allegiance to his brother Henry. Jealous of Richard's lands, young Henry accepted. Joined by Geoffrey, he invaded Poitou. The two brothers banded together and began sacking monasteries, shrines, and rural communities. Then, in the grueling heat of the southern summer, young Henry became ill with dysentery. As he lay dying, his last request was for his father to set his mother free. He died on June 11, 1183. Despite their rocky relationship, King Henry was distraught with grief. He sent a messenger to Eleanor to inform her of their son's death. Eleanor seemed calm when she heard the news, but her grief ran deep. Ten years later, she told the pope the pain of losing of her son still tortured her.

Young Henry's death upset twenty-five years of dynastic planning. Richard was now heir of England, Normandy, Anjou, Poitou, and Aquitaine. The rebellion against him collapsed, but Richard insisted on exacting a vicious punishment. Rebellious nobles and their knights were drowned, blinded, and stabbed as examples to anyone else contemplating rebellion.

Henry was now fifty-three years old, gray, and hobbling from a horse's kick. Eleanor had been his prisoner for ten years, but now he needed her help. He argued with King Philip over lands that Philip insisted belonged to his sister, Marguerite, who was young Henry's widow. Henry disagreed and argued the lands were Eleanor's. She had given them to her son during his lifetime. Eleanor began to appear at Henry's side occasionally to support her claim. She might have resumed her place as queen, but she was not free.

Even after the death of young Henry, Henry's relationship with his remaining sons continued to deteriorate. He still refused to grant them the land and power they desired. Frustrated, Richard and Geoffrey joined forces with King Philip of France and began a series of wars. Although he had no intention of marrying Alys, Richard was further angered because he thought Henry should grant him her dowry, the territory of the Vexin. The ongoing battles began to sap the aging Henry of his will and resources.

In August of 1186, Geoffrey was trampled to death during a tournament, leaving behind his pregnant wife,

Philip II of France. *(Bibliothèque Nationale, Paris)*

Constance of Brittany. Now Henry and Eleanor were left with only two sons.

Henry commissioned a painting of an eagle with four eaglets. Three of the birds were tearing at the parent's back with their talons and beaks. The fourth, also the youngest, was sitting on its neck, waiting to peck at its parent's eyes. "The four young ones of the eagle are my four sons, who will not cease persecuting me even unto death," said Henry. "And the youngest, whom I now embrace with such tender affection, will someday afflict me more grievously and perilously than all the others."

After three years of fighting his sons, Henry was exhausted. He became sick with dysentery and fatigue.

On July 4, 1189, he met with King Philip. Propped up on his horse by his men, Henry wearily agreed to Philip's demands, leaving all of his lands and Alys to Richard and pardoning everyone who had fought against him. But the old man's spirit was still unbroken. "God grant that I may not die until I have had my revenge on you," Henry spat at Richard as he left.

The next day, Henry's adviser looked over the list of vassals who had supported Richard and discovered that John had joined the rebels, too. "Is it true that John, whom I loved beyond all my sons, and for whose gain I have suffered all this misery, has forsaken me? Shame, shame," Henry muttered, "shame on a conquered king."

It was the final blow. The next day, July 6, 1189, Henry died. Four days later, he was buried at Fontevraud. Henry was judged as a harsh, immoral ruler by his contemporaries, but within a decade he was remembered as one of England's greatest medieval kings. After the bitter experience of his son's turbulent reigns, Henry would be judged as an intelligent and firm ruler who had brought peace to a troubled England during his thirty-five-year reign.

Richard was now king. His first act was to order his mother's release. At sixty-seven years old, Eleanor was still strong. She had been held captive for nearly sixteen years and was now ready to make up for lost time.

8

Her Watchful Eye

When Richard's messenger arrived late in the summer of 1189 to release Eleanor, he found the queen already free. When news of Henry's death had reached her she had demanded to be set free at once. Everyone knew how close she was to Richard and did not dare detain her a moment longer.

Eleanor emerged from captivity eager to aid her son in ruling the empire she had helped build. Finally, she had power on her own terms. Richard put her in charge of England. He had only made brief visits to England as a child and did not speak English.

Eleanor sought to build up her son's reputation in England by garnering support from the poor, the wealthy, and the clergy. She freed all captives from prison if they promised to support the new government and to preserve the peace. She also created a more uniform system of coinage, weights, and measures. In Richard's name she relaxed the harshest forest law and pardoned those arrested for poaching in the royal forests. She arranged the marriage of wealthy heiresses to Richard's supporters and revoked Henry's order that the clergy stable and groom the royal horses, an expense that often drained the treasuries of poorer monasteries. Eleanor's efforts all had one aim—to ingratiate Richard with the English people. She did wreak some revenge by imprisoning Alys at Winchester. Eleanor had treated Alys kindly as a child but had been stung by her affair with Henry.

When Richard landed in England he was met with an outpouring of goodwill. Streets were hung with tapestries and garlands. Eleanor had done her job well. On September 3, in a ceremony staged by Eleanor at Westminster Abbey, Richard of Aquitaine became Richard I of England. Usually women were barred from coronations, but Queen Eleanor arranged to be invited by the English nobles. Afterwards, guests enjoyed an extravagant feast and shared endless glasses of wine. Eleanor's other son, John, joined the festivities with his new wife (and cousin) Hawise.

Eleanor had done her best to make Richard loved by his subjects, but his popularity did not last. Richard planned to drain England of money to finance his plans for a Third Crusade.

In the Holy Lands, a new Muslim leader, named Saladin, had succeeded in uniting the Muslim world,

Cp seruse les ordommances du sa
cre au roy richard dangleterre ·

ce autres en chappes de draps dor
brodece de perles deuant lesquels
estuent miteres vini vont riche

A procession during the coronation of Richard I in London, 1189. *(British Library, London)*

which for years had suffered revolt, civil war, and assassinations. Saladin had survived several attempts on his life. He was fired by the idea of a war to drive the European Christians from the eastern Mediterranean coast. Saladin's troops had taken control of Damascus and all of Egypt and surrounded the kingdom of Jerusalem. Then, on October 2, 1187, Saladin invaded Jerusalem to the horror of Christendom. The pope began pleading for another crusade.

Two days after his coronation festivities ended, Richard increased taxes and put everything he could up for sale. He held a national auction for castles, public office, and favors. Eleanor realized her son had inherited little of her political skill or his father's administrative

Saladin was renowned in both the Christian and Muslim worlds for his leadership and military prowess, tempered by his chivalry and merciful nature. Here he is depicted holding a scimitar. *(British Library, London)*

abilities as he recklessly sold off his inheritance. He was determined to sacrifice everything for glory in a holy war. "I would sell all London if I could find a buyer," Richard declared.

The crusade dominated Richard's life and imagination. He was not alone. Crusading fever had enveloped Christendom again. Before the Second Crusade only Edessa had fallen. Now Jerusalem was in the hands of the Turks. Retaking Jerusalem was a sacred duty.

Although Muslims had developed advanced mathematics, explored the movements of the planets and stars, and introduced new metalworking techniques, dances, silks, and spices in advance of Europeans, Richard and the crusaders saw them as infidels. As in Eleanor's youth, gallant men began to talk about taking the cross in village squares and castles. Crusading provided a key to Heaven.

Over fifty years earlier Eleanor had stirred up support for the Second Crusade. It would have been difficult to live in Christendom and not be moved by religious zeal, but certainly the adventure of the journey had appealed to her, just as it now beckoned to her son.

Richard planned for Eleanor to watch his kingdom in his absence. Not trusting John or his half-brother Geoffrey, Richard made them promise to stay out of England for three years. Eleanor, however, persuaded him to release John from this promise, but not Geoffrey. She did not trust Henry's illegitimate son, who was difficult and temperamental. Geoffrey also had no love for his half-brothers, who had rebelled against their father. Eleanor worried Geoffrey might try to usurp the throne while Richard was gone.

Eleanor and Richard both began to think about

succession. If Richard did not return from the crusade, he had no children to succeed him. There was his brother John and Eleanor's three-year-old grandson Arthur, the son of Eleanor's son Geoffrey and his widow Constance. Arthur was born shortly after his father's death and was being raised by his mother in Brittany, a region long hostile to Henry's rule. Eleanor disliked Constance and Arthur, but she had little confidence in John's leadership skills.

Eleanor and Richard made an alliance with King Sancho VI of Navarre, a small kingdom that straddled the Pyrenees Mountains. Sancho had an unmarried daughter, Berengaria, whom he was happy to betroth to Richard. Navarre and France were rivals. To maintain King Philip's friendship, Richard still pretended he would marry Alys after the crusade, but he had little desire to carry through on this promise. Her reputation had been so tarnished by her affair with Henry that Richard and Eleanor no longer considered her a suitable match. To compound matters, there were rumors about Richard's sexual practices. It was said he had once publicly confessed to being a homosexual. Regardless, he needed to take a wife in order to produce an heir to his throne. After Richard and King Philip departed for the Holy Lands, Eleanor was to go to Navarre and collect Berengaria, then meet up with Richard in Sicily, an island off Italy, for the wedding.

On July 4, 1190, the English and French kings began the Third Crusade, leaving together from Vézelay, about three hundred miles east of the kingdom of France. With banners flying, they set off at the head of an immense army. To the cheering crowds, King Richard looked like a lion, sitting atop his stallion on a jeweled saddle. Soon he had the nickname Richard the Lionhearted.

As a child, Richard had been told stories of the Second Crusade and knew how it had been plagued with disaster. He was determined to avoid many of the problems from the Second Crusade by traveling by sea instead of overland, although it was more expensive. More than one hundred ships had been loaded with gold, silver, weapons, and food. This time there were neither women nor troubadours.

This map of Europe during the twelfth century was made in the nineteenth century during a period of renewed interest in the crusades. *(University of Texas, Austin)*

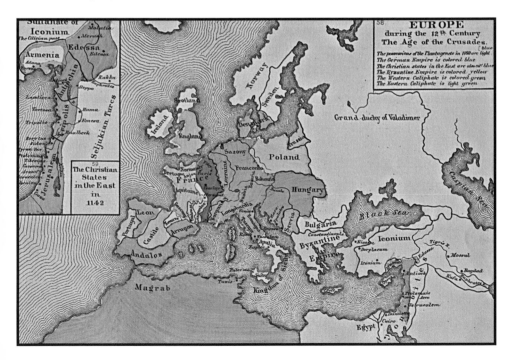

Eleanor headed south to meet Richard's bride, accompanied by a group of attendants from Poitiers. Impatiently, she insisted on crossing the Alps in winter, without considering her age or the possible dangers. Upon arrival, Eleanor collected her son's new wife. Then the two women, along with a large retinue and King Sancho's ambassadors, crossed the Alps and headed into northern Italy before turning south. For several months Eleanor's exact whereabouts were unknown. Eventually, she and Berengaria sailed from Pisa to Sicily.

Philip, who had discovered that Eleanor was headed to meet them with a bride for Richard—which meant Richard was rejecting his sister—tried to prevent Eleanor's ship from docking. When Richard learned of this, he was furious and confronted Philip, who demanded that Richard marry Alys. "Let the King of the English know this for certain, if he puts aside my sister Alys and marries another woman, I will be the enemy of him and his, as long as ever I live," Philip threatened.

Richard told Philip why he could not marry Alys. Although Philip had heard the rumors, he had not believed them. However, when Richard produced witnesses, Philip had no choice but to release him from the betrothal. Richard promised to release Alys from imprisonment and to return her dowry to Philip when they returned from the crusade, but Philip was still bitter when they went their separate ways.

On March 30, 1191, Eleanor and Berengaria landed

in Sicily. There was a great deal for Eleanor and her son to discuss. During her journey, Eleanor had received news that John was attempting to take over England. Eleanor spent only four days in Sicily before returning to Normandy, where she could keep a watchful eye on events in both England and her French territories. On May 12, 1191, Richard and Berengaria were married in Cyprus. Although Berengaria was now queen of England, Eleanor still called herself queen, as did everyone else.

As Eleanor reached Normandy, Richard arrived at Acre, a strategic commercial port near Jerusalem that had been under seige for two years. Richard received a hero's welcome. Knights swam out to meet his ship. In the evening, there was singing and music.

Although he was suffering from malaria, Richard had efficiently reorganized the siege of Acre. Only one month later Acre surrendered, and Richard moved into the royal palace. He was annoyed to find Duke Leopold's flag flying on the roof. The Austrian duke had played little part in helping to recapture the city. Furious, Richard tore down the flag and flung it into the moat. An insulted Leopold withdrew his men from the crusade and swore revenge.

Richard announced that unless the Turks' leader, Saladin, agreed to his terms within a week, he would put every prisoner of war to death. Saladin refused. Richard ordered the mass beheading of nearly 3,000 Turkish men, women, and children. It was an atrocity so great that for hundreds of years afterwards Turkish mothers

The siege of Acre was the deadliest and most important event of the Third Crusade, lasting from August 28, 1189, through July 12, 1191. *(British Library, London)*

disciplined their children with threats of *Malik Ric* or "Evil Richard."

Richard continued his march to Jerusalem, winning victories along the way. Upon his arrival, Richard was forced into bed by malaria. Four weeks later Richard recovered only to discover that most of his allies had fled, including Philip. Jealous over Richard's victories and sick himself with malaria, Philip's hair and nails had fallen out. Suspecting he had been poisoned, Philip returned to France.

Richard fought on, determined to take Jerusalem. Meanwhile, Eleanor warily eyed her other son, John, who was continuing to stir up trouble in England. He traveled around spreading rumors that Richard would never return and claiming that Richard had named him as heir. To make matters worse, when Philip returned to France he told tales of Richard's treachery, hinting that Richard had attempted to poison him. Philip also planned to invade Normandy to punish Richard for not marrying Alys. Eleanor was faced with containing John's ambition in England and maintaining peace in Normandy. She ordered all castles guarding the borders of the Angevin empire to be strengthened and armed, and sent letters to Richard explaining the situation, urging him to come home before his kingdom was lost.

Philip and John banded together to take advantage of Richard's absence. Technically Richard's overlord in

In this image of Richard and Saladin jousting, Saladin is portrayed with a grotesque blue face while Richard's face is hidden by his helmet. *(Courtesy of Art Resource.)*

France, Philip offered John his brother's French territories if John would marry Alys. Although John already had a wife, he agreed and prepared to cross the Channel. Eleanor was warned he was going and managed to get to Portsmouth in time to prevent John from sailing. When she threatened to confiscate all of his lands and castles if he defied her, John backed down. For the moment, Eleanor had achieved a tense peace.

Throughout the spring and summer of 1192, Richard continued fighting for Jerusalem while Eleanor battled on the home front. Tales of Richard's exploits and glorious victories drifted home. In the end, Richard negotiated a truce with Saladin, winning a strip of coastal land and the right for Christians to make pilgrimages to Jerusalem. On September 29, 1192, Richard put his wife on a ship home and followed ten days later. Although the Third Crusade had ended, it had done little for the Christian cause. The Holy City would remain under Muslim rule until the twentieth century. However, the crusaders had succeeded in opening trade with the wealthy Near East. Contact with the educated, civilized Muslims aroused interest in learning, arts, and luxury in Western Europe.

Eleanor expected Richard home by Christmas. As November and December passed and crusaders filtered home, there was no news of Richard. The king was weeks overdue. As Eleanor's lookouts on the coast peered into the fog, messengers waited to race over frozen roads to London with news of the king's landing. Eleanor's silent fears were voiced aloud in alehouses as everyone wondered if the king were alive. People said prayers and lit candles across the country.

Then, in January of 1193, Eleanor heard the news that Richard had been captured by Duke Leopold of Austria while he was passing through Leopold's lands. Leopold's overlord, Holy Roman Emperor Henry VI, was now holding Richard hostage. Henry, a ruthless bully who terrified the German princes, the pope, and cities in northern Italy, knew Richard was a valuable prisoner. Henry also disliked Richard because he had supported his rival, Tancred of Sicily, in a dispute. Richard's father had been his enemy as well.

Eleanor struggled to find Richard. Not knowing his exact location, she sent men to roam villages throughout the Holy Roman Empire, following all leads. Eleanor could not travel to Austria herself and leave England prey to John's scheming. By imprisoning a crusading king, Leopold had violated the Truce of God and shocked Pope Celestine III. The pope excommunicated Leopold and threatened to place an interdict on French lands, preventing people from receiving church services, if Philip invaded Richard's domains.

While Eleanor dealt with Richard's kidnapping, John and Philip worked to keep Richard in captivity. John swaggered around England as its future king, while Eleanor prepared the English coast against Philip's invasion. She ordered people to wield any weapon possible, even plowing tools, to defend their homeland. At

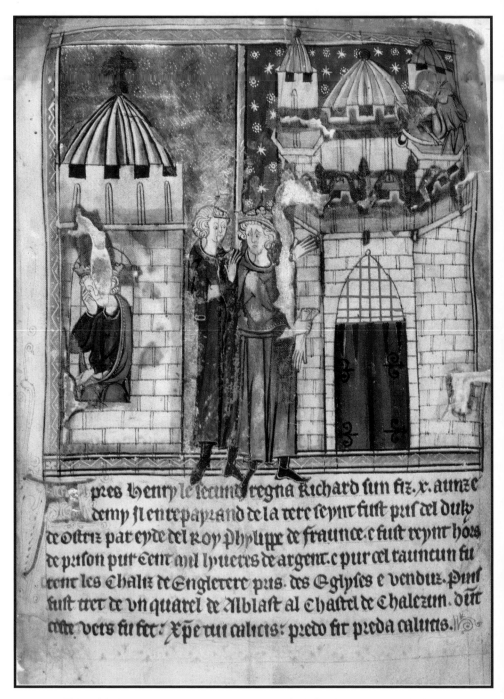

pres henry le setund regna Richard sun fitz. x. aunze demp sl entrepayzand de la terre seynt fust pur cel duk de Ostriz par eyde del Roy Phylyppe de Fraunce. e fust reynt hors de prison pur cent mil lyueres de argent. e pur cel rauncun fu rent les chaliz de Engletere pus. des Eglyses e venduz. puis fust tret de un quarel de Ablast al chastel de Chalezun. dut cete vers su fet: Xpe tui caliceis: predo fit preda caliceis.

Richard the Lionhearted is shown in the center of this illuminated Latin text holding a glove, reluctantly being pushed towards the gate of the prison where he was held by Holy Roman Emperor Henry VI. *(Courtesy of Art Resource.)*

the same time she worked to win Richard's release.

Eventually, Richard's location was discovered. One legend said that his favorite minstrel had discovered his whereabouts by roaming Austria. The minstrel would stop outside castles and sing songs he and Richard had composed together. One day, the story went, he heard King Richard's voice singing back from high above. Richard was being held in a fortress on a steep slope near Vienna, Austria, which was guarded day and night.

Two of Eleanor's men returned after meeting Henry VI. They warned her that the emperor would demand a huge ransom for Richard. Eleanor wrote to Pope Celestine III, who had promised three times to intervene. Eleanor wrote angry letters, berating him for not taking action. Richard was a crusader under the Church's protection. She wrote:

> I am all anxiety, both within and without, whence my very words are full of suffering. . . . Two sons yet survive to my comfort, who now live only to distress me, a miserable and condemned creature. King Richard is detained in bonds, and his brother John depopulates the captive's kingdom with the sword and lays it waste with fire. Restore my son to me, then, O man of God, if indeed you are a man of God and not a man of mere blood.

Eleanor signed the letter, "Eleanor, by the wrath of God, Queen of England."

The eighty-seven-year-old pope was afraid to interfere

in the situation. For years, the papacy and the Holy Roman Empire had been in conflict. The pope did not want to incur the wrath of an emperor whose armies surrounded papal territory and who had recently slit the throats of the pope's ambassadors.

John continued to stir up rebellion, demanding that the English nobles declare him king. Backed by Eleanor, Richard's advisers refused. As Philip invaded Normandy, he and John tried to bribe Henry to keep Richard in prison. The emperor refused, not wanting to further their territorial ambitions. But Henry was demanding a ransom of 100,000 marks (two times England's annual revenue), several nobles' sons as hostages, as well as Richard's help overthrowing Tancred of Sicily. Richard and Eleanor had little choice but to agree.

Once the ransom terms were set, Richard was treated more like a guest than a prisoner. He received visitors from England and developed friendships with many German princes. When he heard about John's treachery, he remarked, "My brother John is not the man to conquer a country if there is anyone to offer the feeblest resistance." Richard was unconcerned and confident he would be home soon.

Eleanor set to work raising the ransom money. Most people gave willingly. John made a show of helping but stole the money he collected to fund his schemes. Anticipating Richard's freedom, Philip warned John, "The devil has been let loose!" John abandoned his plans in England and fled to Paris. Eleanor then persuaded her

English advisers to confiscate John's lands and castles and convinced the pope to excommunicate him and Philip for violating the Truce of God and attempting to seize Richard's kingdom.

In October, Eleanor's messengers took some of the money to the emperor. She would deliver the rest of the money and the hostages by January 17, 1194. But when she arrived in Austria she found the emperor had postponed Richard's release. Philip and John had bribed Henry to either deliver Richard to them or to hold him for another year. Richard's German friends protested this change. After days of negotiations, the emperor agreed to release Richard as long as Richard acknowledged him as the overlord of England. It meant that Richard technically would be Henry's vassal. Eleanor realized this was a humiliating act, but it was a meaningless gesture, and Richard's only choice. She encouraged him to submit, and on February 4 Richard was released. Eleanor broke down in tears as she and her son headed home.

"The news of the coming of the king, so long and so desperately awaited, flew faster than the north wind," wrote William of Newburgh, a medieval chronicler. The news extinguished the last of John's support, and celebrations ensued. Eleanor and Richard triumphantly arrived in England a month later.

They stayed briefly before sailing for Normandy, anxious to recover the lands Philip had seized. Neither one of them would ever return to England. Once in Normandy, Eleanor took steps to reconcile her two sons.

She summoned John to appear before Richard. When John fell at his brother's feet and wept, Richard forgave him. "Think no more of it, John. You are but a child and were left to evil counselors. Your advisors shall pay for this," Richard said. For the next five years, John humbly remained loyal to Richard.

Richard's capture and the raising of his ransom had exhausted Eleanor. At seventy-two, she had preserved her son's kingdom and rescued him from enemies. She had ruled alone for eighteen turbulent months. Now she wanted to rest. She retired to the abbey of Fontevraud, where the silvery Vienne River wound its way through the valleys and dark forests. She took refuge in these familiar surroundings. Her grandmother and husband Henry were buried there. Eleanor lived in the abbey as a guest rather than a nun.

Eleanor's next few years were quiet. Life changed little at Fontevraud. She kept a careful eye on Richard's lands and arranged the marriage of her daughter Joanna, whose husband had died, to Raymond VI of Toulouse. Thirty-five-year-old Alys married one of her brother's vassals. Richard still had no heir. Although he was married to Berengaria, they had lived separately since their marriage. Eleanor outlived both of her daughters with Louis and saw her grandson, Otto, elected as the Holy Roman Emperor upon Henry VI's sudden death. The struggle over power in France continued with skirmishes here and there, but with few results.

Despite famine and a shortage of money, Richard

built one of the greatest medieval castles. To ward off future attacks on Normandy, Château Gaillard, the "Saucy Castle," was built on a mighty rock in the Seine River. The fortress, which took three years to build, was said to be unbreakable. When jealous Philip looked upon its walls, he declared, "If its walls were made of solid iron, yet would I take them."

When Richard heard this, he said, "By God's throat, if its walls were made of butter, yet would I hold them!" Richard held an iron grip over England and his domains in France.

A few months after moving into Château Gaillard, Richard left for southern France. He wanted to seize some treasure that was rumored to have been discovered by a farmer. Rumors about a pot of Roman coins grew until it became a golden statue of an emperor. Richard was enthralled with the stories. When the farmer's overlord, Aymar, Count of Limoges, kept the treasure from him, Richard decided to travel to Châlus, where he laid siege to Aymar's castle.

The siege had gone on for nearly three weeks when one evening Richard, without putting on his armor, rode out to work with the engineers who were attempting to dig under the castle's walls. According to an account written by Roger of Hoveden, a man named Bertram de Gurdun, who was inside the castle, let loose an arrow that struck Richard in the arm.

When one of Richard's knights tried to pull the arrow out, the wooden shaft broke off and the metal arrowhead remained in his arm. It took a butcher hours to get the arrow out of his arm, but only after he had "carelessly mangled the King's arm in every part," said Roger of Hoveden.

The bandaged wound was soon raw and swollen and became infected. Richard knew he was dying. After the castle fell, he demanded that Bertram de Gurdun be brought to him. When Richard asked why Bertram had wanted to kill him, Bertram replied: "You slew my father and my two brothers with your own hand, and you had intended now to kill me. Therefore take any revenge on me that you may think fit, for I will readily endure the greatest torments that you can devise, so long as you have met with your end, having inflicted evils so many and so great upon the world." Richard was reputedly so moved by Bertram's forthrightness and bravery that he ordered he not be punished. But once Richard was dead Bertram was flayed alive and hanged.

Richard also summoned Eleanor, who rode day and night to reach his bedside. On April 6, 1199, Richard died in his mother's arms.

Richard's death was a terrible blow to Eleanor. He had bequeathed his kingdom to his brother John. Although she had lost her favorite son, there was little time for grieving. Eleanor needed to put aside her sorrows and come out of retirement. She still had one son left and she needed to help maintain the Angevin empire.

9

The Empire Crumbles

Eleanor kept the news of Richard's death secret until she could notify John, who was, ironically, visiting Arthur, the other claimant to the throne, in Brittany. Most men and women learned of Richard's death when they saw the royal funeral procession pass by in the late spring of 1199.

No one was certain who would become king. Richard's deathbed naming of John as his heir was influential but not decisive. The rules of hereditary succession were unclear; John and his nephew Arthur both had strong claims.

For Eleanor, the most important question was not which of the remaining heirs had the best claim, but rather who would make the less objectionable king. She had little confidence in either man and chose John, apparently, as the lesser of two evils. She sent him to take possession of the royal treasure and demanded that Richard's court swear allegiance to him.

Eleanor was aware of her son's fickle, self-centered, and undisciplined nature. Winning him the throne would be a battle and a thankless task, as illustrated by his behavior when he visited Richard's tomb at Fontevraud. During the bishop's sermon at the abbey, John grew impatient and demanded three times that the bishop end the sermon so he could have dinner. The congregation, which included Eleanor, was horrified when John began to jingle gold coins in his pocket. He had brought them to offer the bishop during the service. Before he tossed them into the collection plate, John sneered, "I am considering these gold pieces and thinking that, if I had had them a few days ago, I should not have given them to you, but swept them into my own wallet." He laughed at the bishop's anger.

The same day, only thirty miles away, Arthur and his mother, Constance, were on the march with an army from Brittany. They had taken Angers, where a gathering of nobles had accepted Arthur as their king. Arthur also had King Philip's support. Philip had taken Arthur in as a boy and raised him with his own son.

Both England and Normandy had accepted John's succession to the throne. Before his coronation in England, John traveled to Normandy. As Normandy was ruled by a duke, John was proclaimed the duke of Normandy. During the solemn ceremony he laughed with his friends and made jokes. When presented with the duke's lance, John was so busy giggling with his friends that he dropped it. Everyone interpreted this as an omen.

Eleanor raised an army and went to recover Angers from Arthur. The aged queen caught Arthur and Constance off-guard, and they hastily retreated. But the fight was not over. Brittany was lost and Anjou, Maine, and Tourraine were within Arthur's grasp despite Eleanor's best efforts. Even Aquitaine remained vulnerable.

Eleanor set off on a tour of her lands. She gave away castles and privileges to people who pledged loyalty. She dispensed justice and addressed old grievances. She even gave away Talmont, her family's ancient seaside hunting lodge. Eleanor shrewdly released towns from their feudal obligations. The number of cities had increased dramatically during Eleanor's life and many of them were now clamoring to break free of ancient ties. She gave many of the cities charters making them independent. The charters outlined the conditions under which the cities were organized. These towns were no longer tied to the nearby noblility for protection. Nor were the inhabitants required to pay homage or offer up a percentage of their crops to safeguard themselves from attack. But they now needed to contribute to their own defense. The granting of freedoms to towns signaled the beginning of the end of the feudal system. Eleanor hoped these new towns, which now had a stake in their own protection, would help impose law and organization throughout Aquitaine. Soon King Philip began implementing a similar policy.

Between April and July Eleanor traveled more than a thousand miles. She also swallowed her pride and paid homage to King Philip for her lands of Poitou and Aquitaine, recognizing him as her overlord. With this act she declared her lands separate from the long struggle between the Plantagenets and the Capets. This robbed Philip and Arthur of the excuse to attack her territory.

Two months later, Eleanor gave these properties to John. After paying homage to Philip, she had the right to make her son her heir to these lands, and there was little Philip could do about it. But her gift meant that John now controlled a considerable amount of territory and was a more powerful adversary. Although John and Philip had been allies before, now Philip viewed him as a potential threat. As John's position was growing stronger, Arthur's was weakening. John's troops had Arthur and his mother on the run.

While Eleanor was drumming up support, John was crowned in England at Westminster Abbey on May 27, 1199. He had his marriage to Hawise annulled and began seeking a better marriage. Eleanor was joined by her daughter Joanna, who was pregnant but in poor health. She soon died at Fontevraud. Once again Eleanor had to bury a child. Of her ten children, only two remained living—John and her namesake Eleanor, who lived in the faraway kingdom of Castile.

In the meantime Philip and Arthur had fallen out.

JOHN.

King John of England. (Cassell's History of England, *1902*)

Philip was involved in a tangle with the Church over his
marriage and could not afford to have John as an enemy
any longer. In January of 1200, he and John concluded

a truce in which Philip recognized John as Richard's heir, and John paid Philip a fee. The truce also provided that Philip's son would marry one of Eleanor's grand-daughters from Castile. Eleanor would travel to Spain to retrieve the bride. Although Eleanor was seventy-seven years old, she looked forward to being reunited with her daughter, whom she had not seen for nearly thirty years.

Eleanor set off to fetch the young bride, crossing the Pyrenees Mountains during winter and then traveling on to Castile. For two months, Eleanor enjoyed visiting her daughter's sophisticated court. Her daughter had helped spread southern French culture to Spain. In late March, Eleanor set off for home again, accompanied by her granddaughter, sixteen-year-old Princess Blanche. They returned to Bordeaux, where an escort met them. The trip was lengthy and tiresome for Eleanor, who decided she could not continue. She headed home to Fontevraud, while Blanche was escorted to Normandy.

Eleanor intended to spend the rest of her days at Fontevraud, but John soon made a decision that forced Eleanor out again. Her thirty-three-year-old son had become smitten with a thirteen-year-old beauty named Isabella. Although Isabella was already betrothed to Hugh de Lusignan, the scion of a powerful family, her father encouraged the match with King John. But Eleanor knew it was a mistake for John to marry Isabella. John would not listen and married her anyway. Isabella was crowned queen of England on October 8, 1200.

The wedding was a severe insult to the honor of the

powerful Lusignan family. Ironically, in later years, Isabella grew to hate John. Although she bore him five children, it was said that she became an "evil-minded, adulterous, dangerous woman."

It took some time for the consequences of John's impulsive marriage to develop. However, in 1201, Hugh de Lusignan made a protest to King Philip, John's overlord. Philip summoned John to answer the charges, but John refused to appear.

Meanwhile, Philip and Arthur had mended their differences and allied with other nobles in southern France who were upset about John's marriage. Philip seized on John's refusal to honor the summons and confiscated his French territories. He also declared their truce broken, attacked Normandy, and sent Arthur to take Anjou, Maine, Tourraine, and Poitou. John was not prepared to fight a war throughout his realm.

An outraged Eleanor traveled to Poitiers. When Arthur learned of Eleanor's location, he besieged her castle, intending to take his grandmother hostage. The castle's defenses were weak. Eleanor smuggled out messengers with orders for John to send her aid. She then stalled by dragging out surrender negotiations with Arthur. Eventually Eleanor was forced to lock herself in the keep while Arthur's men breached the outer walls of the castle.

Once John received news of Eleanor's plight he set out with his army. They marched day and night, covering eighty miles in two days. He arrived soon after dawn on August 1, 1202. John and his army attacked, catching

Arthur's men by surprise. They killed nearly every man and captured Arthur. Eleanor was unharmed.

Even by medieval standards, John treated his prisoners appallingly. Many of them starved to death in prison. Arthur himself was locked in a dungeon in Normandy. Eleanor pleaded with John not to harm him. She knew the mistreatment of the prisoners would cause a public outcry.

At eighty years old, Eleanor longed for the peace of Fontevraud. She returned to the abbey and became a nun. For sixty-six years, Eleanor had been a queen, first of France and then of England. She had lived during a time when there were many changes in the medieval world.

At the beginning of Eleanor's life, books were rare. Most were religious and written in Latin. During her life there was an increase in the number of books written in languages other than Latin and on nonreligious subjects. Verse and prose took on new, popular forms, and libraries expanded as reading became a leisure activity for more people. Stories that had circulated orally for hundreds of years were written down. Arthurian tales of love, fire, and blood sparked imagination.

Along with the literature fueled by Eleanor's troubadours and an increasingly educated clergy came the growth of schools. Universities brought prestige to cities such as Paris. Schooling in feudal Europe had been scarce, but as urban centers expanded, the newly emerging merchant class created a demand for skilled writers and account keepers.

Eleanor's reign also had seen some improvement in the rights of women. Helped by the chivalrous tunes of troubadours, women were seen as wielding power in love, at least. New Gothic cathedrals were raised and dedicated to Mary in the midst of the cult of chivalry and of the Virgin Mary. These ideals of religion and courtly love represented how women wanted society to be. But change was slow. Most women were still seen as property, primarily needed to bear children.

An economic transformation had begun to sweep over Europe during the twelfth century. Commerce was revived, due in part to the travels of the crusaders. Gradually, money was reintroduced to an economy that had been hampered by the barter system. Towns sprang up in the shadows of great churches and castles that provided a market for specialization. Merchants began to trade in specific commodities. Northern Europe began importing wool from England to cloth makers in Flanders. Valuable wines imported from France triggered a boom in domestic wine production. Trade routes stimulated by the crusades created commerce and increased wealth across the continent. Sugar, silks, and spices arrived in the Mediterranean from eastern trading ports such as Baghdad and Damascus. Through the interaction with faraway cultures, crusaders brought back new clothing, jewelry, literature, and games such as chess.

In France, Eleanor rested, but outside her abbey walls the chaos of the collapsing Angevin empire continued. By Christmas, rumors were circulating that Arthur was

Pietàs, pieces of art depicting the Virgin Mary cradling the body of Christ, reflect the cult of Mary that developed during Eleanor's lifetime. *(Rheinische Landesmuseum, Bonn)*

dead. People said John had drunkenly pushed him off a cliff. By the end of March it was clear Arthur had vanished. Whatever really happened to Arthur, John was universally condemned and Arthur's supporters rose up in revolt. John's disgruntled vassals defected, yet again, to Philip.

John faced a nearly impossible task. He had to hold together the vast Angevin empire, but his cruelty and deceit had alienated those who could have helped him. At first he stubbornly refused to act, then made erratic attempts to recover his losses. Everyone lost faith in him completely.

Philip made serious inroads into Normandy. On March 6, 1204, Château Gaillard fell. This was the death knell of the Angevin empire. Soon all of Normandy would follow, and then Poitou. Fortunately, Eleanor did not live to see its complete destruction.

Eleanor of Aquitaine died at Fontevraud on April 1, 1204. She lived to be eighty-two years old, a remarkable feat in medieval times. Amidst the chaos of the collapse of her life's work, she died quietly. Her death went virtually unnoticed. She was buried between her husband Henry and her son Richard. A beautiful stone effigy was made to commemorate her. On it she is lying down with her crown on her head. There is a hint of a smile on her lips and a book open in her hands. "She graced the nobility of her birth with the honesty of her life, enriched it with her moral excellence, and adorned it with the flowers of her virtues; and by her renown for

King John and the Magna Carta

Even before Eleanor died in 1204, John had lost control of most of Normandy, the original Plantagenet holding. He continued fruitlessly fighting King Philip, attempting to reclaim his French possessions. John pitilessly taxed his citizens to pay for his failed military expeditions, which followed the huge sums Richard had already extracted to pay for the crusades. John resorted to seizing the property and revenue produced by the lands managed by his vassals, and found other ways to be repressive and to govern in an arbitrary manner.

In 1214, after another failed attempt to retake Normandy, John returned to England, where he was met by a rebellion of England's most powerful barons. John sent William Marshall, the most respected knight in England, to listen to the barons' complaints, but when William returned with his report John refused to negotiate. Instead, he demanded total subservience. Enraged, the barons formed an army and seized London. It was soon obvious John did not have a chance to win on the battlefield. He dispatched Marshall to the barons again, this time with a message that he would grant their demands.

On June 15, 1215, King John met the barons at Runnymede—a pleasant meadow by the Thames River—and signed the Magna Carta, a document that limited the king's power, provided a new system of courts, and promised that no Englishman could be put in prison without a trial.

Soon after the signing, John broke the terms of the Magna Carta and returned to the battlefield against the barons. The king marched around England, leaving destruction in his wake but avoiding a decisive battle. The barons, meanwhile, received aid from the French by offering the English crown to Louis, King Philip's son, who soon crossed the English Channel with an army. After several months of fighting, King John fell ill and died in 1216. After his death, William Marshall had

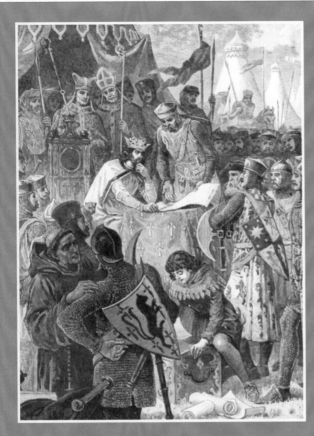

King John signs the Magna Carta. *(Cassell's History of England, 1902)*

John's nine-year-old son Henry III crowned king to avoid letting the throne fall into Louis's hands, and served as his regent until Henry was old enough to assume the throne.

In one respect the Magna Carta, which was intended to keep the king within the bounds established by feudalism, was inherently conservative. The nobles were seeking to restore what they saw as the proper relationship between the king and the nobility. But the Magna Carta was also forward-looking. As a written document that attempted to constrain the king's power, it implicitly contained the core constitutional principle of a government guided by law and not an individual's capricious decisions. It was a first, tentative step toward the establishment of a constitutional monarchy.

Eleanor's effigy at Fontevraud Abbey portrays her as a pious yet learned woman.
(Courtesy of Art Resource.)

unmatched goodness, she surpassed almost all the queens of the world," wrote the nuns at Fontevraud.

Eleanor has been called the grandmother of Europe. Her sons ruled England and large sections of modern France, and her daughters were queens of Sicily and Castile. Two of her grandsons were Holy Roman Emperors, and her descendants were kings and queens of England, France, Portugal, Scotland, Castile, and Jerusalem.

Although legends swirled around her, her fame rests on her actions and her long and controversial role in politics. She ruled as capably as any man in a time when women held neither rights nor power. Eleanor of Aquitaine refused to accept the destiny that men handed to her and is remembered today as a medieval queen of grace and strength.

Timeline

1122   Eleanor of Aquitaine is born either in Poitiers or Bordeaux, France.

1130   Mother Aenor and brother William die.

1137   Father William dies; inherits Aquitaine and Poitou; marries Louis Capet, heir to the throne of France; King Louis VI of France dies; husband Louis becomes king of France; crowned queen of France.

1145   First daughter, Marie, is born.

1147   Takes the cross at St. Denis with Louis, and the Second Crusade begins.

1148   The Turks attack the crusading army, and the Second Crusade ends in failure.

1150   Second daughter, Alix, is born.

1152   Divorced from Louis; travels home to Poitiers; married to Henry on May 18.

1153   First son, William, is born.

1154   King Stephen of England dies; Henry and Eleanor are crowned King and Queen of England.

1155   Second son, Henry, is born; Thomas Becket becomes chancellor.

1156   Three-year-old William dies; third daughter, Matilda, is born.

1157   Third son, Richard, is born.

1158   Fourth son, Geoffrey, is born.

1160   Young Henry marries Louis's three-year-old daughter.

1161   Fourth daughter, Eleanor, is born.

1162   Thomas Becket becomes the Archbishop of Canterbury.

1164   Fifth daughter, Joanna, is born; Eleanor and Louis's two daughters, Marie and Alix, are married.

1166   Discovers Henry's mistress, Rosamund de Clifford; fifth son, John, is born.

1167   Daughter Matilda marries Duke Henry the Lion; leaves Henry to live permanently in Poitiers.

1169   Henry divides his empire in the Treaty of Montmirail; Richard is betrothed to Louis's daughter Alys.

1170   Richard becomes the duke of Aquitaine; Young Henry crowned as future king of England; Thomas Becket murdered at Canterbury Cathedral.

1172   The pope makes Becket a saint.

1173   Young Henry escapes his father and joins Louis in rebellion, along with Richard and Geoffrey; Eleanor is captured and imprisoned by Henry.

1174   Moved to England and held in captivity for the next decade; sons' rebellion ends.

1175   Refuses to consent to an annulment and to enter a convent.

1176   Daughter Joanna marries King William of Sicily; Rosamund de Clifford dies.

1177   Daughter Eleanor marries the King of Castile.

1180   King Louis of France dies and is succeeded by his son Philip.

1181   Geoffrey marries Constance of Brittany.

1183   Richard, Geoffrey, and young Henry at war with each other over Aquitaine; young Henry dies of illness.

1186   Geoffrey dies at a tournament in Paris.

1187   The Turks invade and take Jerusalem, prompting another crusade.

1188 Henry and Philip at war.

1189 Henry dies after surrendering; Eleanor's daughter, Matilda, dies. John marries his cousin Hawise; Richard is crowned king of England.

1190 Richard and Philip leave on the Third Crusade.

1191 Eleanor and Berengaria meet Richard in Italy; Richard and Berengaria are married.

1192 The Third Crusade ends.

1193 Learns of Richard's capture and raises his ransom.

1194 Travels to Austria and frees Richard.

1197 Daughter Alix dies.

1198 Daughter Marie dies.

1199 Richard dies of an arrow wound; John is crowned king of England; Joanna dies in childbirth.

1200 Travels to Castile to fetch her granddaughter to marry Philip's son; John marries Isabella of Angoulême; Isabella is crowned queen of England.

1202 John and Philip go to war; Eleanor travels to Poitiers and is besieged by her grandson, Arthur; John rescues Eleanor, and Arthur is captured.

1203 Arthur apparently is murdered.

1204 Philip captures Normandy; Eleanor dies at eighty-two years old.

Sources

CHAPTER ONE: The Other Aenor

p. 14, "Opulent Aquitaine . . ." Weir, Alison, *Eleanor of Aquitaine: A Life* (New York: Ballantine Publishing Group, 1999), 5.

p. 15, "From the fury . . ." Brooks, Polly Schoyer, *Queen Eleanor: Independent Spirit of the Medieval World* (New York: Houghton Mifflin, 1999), 2.

p. 25, "To live with . . ." Seward, Desmond, *Eleanor of Aquitaine: The Mother Queen* (New York: Dorset Press, 1978), 25.

p. 25, "a clod of dung" Ibid., 201.

CHAPTER TWO: Queen of France

p. 42, "He loved . . ." Ibid., 30.

p. 44, "Fie on . . ." Weir, *Eleanor of Aquitaine: A Life*, 34.

p. 50, "For from whom except . . ." Kelly, Amy, *Eleanor of Aquitaine and the Four Kings* (Cambridge, MA: Harvard University Press, 1966), 24.

p. 51-3, "No one would . . ." Ibid., 26.

p. 53, "My child . . ." Meade, Marion, *Eleanor of Aquitaine: A Biography* (New York: Penguin Books, 1991), 66.

CHAPTER THREE: Journey to Jerusalem

p. 61, "Crosses, crosses . . ." Brooks, *Queen Eleanor: Independent Spirit of the Medieval World*, 33.

p. 61, "To Jerusalem . . ." Weir, *Eleanor of Aquitaine: A Life,* 49.

p. 61, "I opened my mouth . . ." Seward, *Eleanor of Aquitaine: The Mother Queen,* 42.

p. 63, "Anyone seeing . . ." Kelly, *Eleanor of Aquitaine: and the Four Kings,* 37.

p. 65, "The Lord is . . ." Weir, *Eleanor of Aquitaine: A Life,* 56.

p. 70, "His constant . . ." Ibid., 64.

p. 72, "It would be . . ." Owen, D.D.R., *Eleanor of Aquitaine: Queen and Legend* (Cambridge, MA: Blackwell Publishers, 1996), 104.

p. 73, "Their mutual anger . . ." Weir, *Eleanor of Aquitaine: A Life,* 67.

p. 74, "was not able . . ." Meade, *Eleanor of Aquitaine: A Biography,* 119.

p. 74, "It remains a mystery . . ." Weir, *Eleanor of Aquitaine: A Life,* 72.

CHAPTER FOUR: A New Life

p. 80, "at crack of . . ." Weir, *Eleanor of Aquitaine: A Life,* 83.

p. 84, "the floodgates of heaven . . ." Meade, *Eleanor of Aquitaine: A Biography,* 161.

p. 86, "You have been . . ." Seward, *Eleanor of Aquitaine: The Mother Queen,* 73.

p. 86, "a man beyond hope . . ." Ibid., 73.

p. 88, "where he was received . . ." Weir, *Eleanor of Aquitaine: A Life,* 100.

p. 89, "come without delay . . ." Meade, *Eleanor of Aquitaine: A Biography,* 165.

CHAPTER FIVE: Queen of England

p. 93, "Long live the king!" Weir, *Eleanor of Aquitaine: A Life,* 103.

p. 98, "The king and Becket . . ." Meade, *Eleanor of Aquitaine: A Biography,* 175.

p. 100, "Now in Ireland . . ." Weir, *Eleanor of Aquitaine: A Life,* 124.

p. 101, "The eagle of . . ." Owen, *Eleanor of Aquitaine: Queen and Legend,* 113.

p. 103, "Here lies Arthur . . ." Weir, *Eleanor of Aquitaine: A Life*, 131.

p. 104, "The king would . . ." Meade, *Eleanor of Aquitaine: A Biography, 188.*

p. 105-106, "Marvelous is the . . ." Weir, *Eleanor of Aquitaine: A Life,* 148.

p. 112, "The love which . . ." Meade, *Eleanor of Aquitaine: A Biography,* 210.

CHAPTER SIX: Betrayal and Murder

p. 114, "a hair shirt . . ." Weir, *Eleanor of Aquitaine: A Life,* 156.

p. 115, "By the eyes of God! . . ." Meade, *Eleanor of Aquitaine: A Biography,* 218.

p. 117, "We have not . . ." Ibid., 226.

p. 117, "The king . . ." Weir, *Eleanor of Aquitaine: A Life,* 163.

p. 126, "Come my archbishop . . ." Kelly, *Eleanor of Aquitaine and the Four Kings,* 145.

p. 127, "My lord, while Thomas . . ." Weir, *Eleanor of Aquitaine: A Life,* 186.

p. 127, "Will no one rid me . . ." Warren, W.L., *Henry II* (Berkeley, CA: University of California Press, 1973), 601.

p. 129, "Where is Thomas . . ." Weir, *Eleanor of Aquitaine: A Life.,* 187.

p. 129, "Let us away . . ." Ibid., 188.

CHAPTER SEVEN: Rebellion

p. 135, "I advise you king . . ." Weir, *Eleanor of Aquitaine: A Life,* 199.

p. 136, "Return, O illustrious . . ." Brooks, *Queen Eleanor: Independent Spirit of the Medieval World,* 118.

p. 139, "The king, who had . . ." Weir, *Eleanor of Aquitaine, A Life,* 213.

p. 140, "Foul as it is . . ." Ibid., 233.

p. 143, "The four young ones . . ." Warren, *Henry II,* 601.

p. 144, "God grant . . ." Owen, *Eleanor of Aquitaine: Queen and Legend,* 78.

p. 144, "Is it true . . ." Kelly, *Eleanor of Aquitaine and the Four Kings,* 245.

CHAPTER EIGHT: Her Watchful Eye

p. 148, "I would sell . . ." Brooks, *Queen Eleanor: Independent Spirit of the Medieval World,* 134.

p. 152, "Let the king . . ." Kelly, *Eleanor of Aquitaine and the Four Kings,* 261.

p. 154, "Evil Richard" Weir, *Eleanor of Aquitaine: A Life,* 268.

p. 159, "I am all anxiety . . ." Ibid., 283-285.

p. 160, "My brother John . . ." Ibid., 292.

p. 160, "The devil has been . . ." Seward, *Eleanor of Aquitaine: The Mother Queen,* 177.

p. 161, "The news of . . ." Kelly, *Eleanor of Aquitaine and the Four Kings,* 319.

p. 162, "Think no more . . ." Meade, *Eleanor of Aquitaine: A Biography,* 324-325.

p. 163, "If its walls were . . ." Weir, *Eleanor of Aquitaine: A Life,* 305.

p. 164, "carelessly mangled the . . ." Ibid., 310.

p. 164, "You slew my . . ." Ibid., 310-311.

CHAPTER NINE: The Empire Crumbles

p. 166, "I am considering . . ." Kelly, *Eleanor of Aquitaine and the Four Kings,* 348.

p. 171, "evil minded, adulterous . . ." Weir, *Eleanor of Aquitaine,* 328.

p. 175, "She graced . . ." Ibid., 344.

Bibliography

Brooks, Polly Schoyer. *Queen Eleanor: Independent Spirit of the Medieval World.* New York: Houghton Mifflin, 1983.

Cantor, Norman F. *Civilization of the Middle Ages.* New York: HarperCollins, 1993.

Chamberlin, E. R. *Life in Medieval France.* New York: G. P. Putnam's Sons, 1967.

Davies, Norman. *Europe: A History.* New York: Oxford University, 1996.

Gies, Joseph and Francis Gies. *Daily Life in Medieval Times.* New York: Black Dog & Leventhal, 1990.

Hanawalt, Barbara A. *The Middle Ages: An Illustrated History.* New York: Oxford University Press, 1998.

Holmes, Urban Tigner, Jr. *Daily Living in the Twelfth Century.* Madison, WI: University of Wisconsin Press, 1966.

Konstam, Angus. *Atlas of Medieval Europe.* New York: Thalamus, 2000.

Kelly, Amy. *Eleanor of Aquitaine and the Four Kings.* Cambridge, MA: Harvard University Press, 1966.

Larrington, Carolyne. *Women and Writing in Medieval Europe.* New York: Routledge, 1995.

Meade, Marion. *Eleanor of Aquitaine: A Biography.* New York: Penguin, 1977.

National Geographic Society. *The Age of Chivalry.* Washington, D.C.: National Geographic Society, 1969.

Owen, D.D.R. *Eleanor of Aquitaine: Queen and Legend.* Cambridge, MA: Blackwell, 1996.

Seward, Desmond. *Eleanor of Aquitaine: The Mother Queen.* New York: Dorset, 1978.

Warren, W.L., *Henry II.* Berkeley, CA: University of California Press, 1973.

Weir, Alison. *Eleanor of Aquitaine.* New York: Ballantine Books, 1999.

Web sites

http://www.royal.gov.uk
The official Web site of the British monarchy. These pages contain information about the history of the monarchy, including a complete listing of the kings and queens of England and Britain, with brief biographies.

http://www.fordham.edu/halsall/sbook1k.html
An extensive overview of every crusade, including the successes and failures of each. Also provides original correspondence regarding the crusades.

http://cunnan.sca.org.au/wiki/Troubadour
Detailed history of the troubadours, including an exploration of their poetic and musical styles, as well as details about the lives of various famous troubadours.

http://www.languedoc-france.info/1006_occitan.htm
An interesting history of Occitan, the language of Eleanor and the troubadours, dispelling the idea that it was a patios (or corrupt) form of the French language.

http://www.bbc.co.uk/history/state/church_reformation/becket_01.shtml
Features many articles on the life and times of Thomas Becket, with a variety of religious images.

Index

189